J   4328423
937   14.95
Ste
Steffens
The fall of the Roman Empire

DATE DUE			

LF

GREAT RIVER REGIONAL LIBRARY

St. Cloud, Minnesota 56301

GAYLORD MG

GREAT MYSTERIES

The Fall of the Roman Empire

OPPOSING VIEWPOINTS®

Look for these and other exciting *Great Mysteries: Opposing Viewpoints* books:

GREAT MYSTERIES

The Fall of the Roman Empire

OPPOSING VIEWPOINTS®

by Bradley Steffens

Greenhaven Press, Inc.   P.O. Box 289009, San Diego, California 92198-9009

Library of Congress Cataloging-in-Publication Data

Steffens, Bradley, 1956-
    The fall of the Roman Empire : opposing viewpoints / by Bradley Steffens.
        p. cm. — (Great mysteries)
    Includes bibliographical references and index.
    Summary: Presents opposing viewpoints on the fall of the Roman Empire and its causes.
    ISBN 1-56510-098-0
    1. Rome—History—Empire, 284-476—Juvenile literature.
    [1. Rome—History—Empire, 284-476.]   I. Title.   II. Series:
Great mysteries (Saint Paul, Minn.)
DG311.S77   1994
937'.06—dc20   93-11025
                                                    CIP
                                                        AC

For Betsy Crawford,
whose love of history inspired my own.

Contents

Introduction

This book is written for the curious—those who want to explore the mysteries that are everywhere. To be human is to be constantly surrounded by wonderment. How do birds fly? Are ghosts real? Can animals and people communicate? Was King Arthur a real person or a myth? Why did Amelia Earhart disappear? Did history really happen the way we think it did? Where did the world come from? Where is it going?

Great Mysteries: Opposing Viewpoints books are intended to offer the reader an opportunity to explore some of the many mysteries that both trouble and intrigue us. For the span of each book, we want the reader to feel that he or she is a scientist investigating the extinction of the dinosaurs, an archaeologist searching for clues to the origin of the great Egyptian pyramids, a psychic detective testing the existence of ESP.

One thing all mysteries have in common is that there is no ready answer. Often there are *many* answers but none on which even the majority of authorities agrees. *Great Mysteries: Opposing Viewpoints* books introduce the intriguing views of the experts, allowing the reader to participate in their explorations, their theories, and their disagreements as they try to explain the mysteries of our world.

But most readers won't want to stop here. These *Great Mysteries: Opposing Viewpoints* aim to stimulate the reader's curiosity. Although truth is often impossible to discover, the search is fascinating. It is up to the reader to examine the evidence, to decide whether the answer is there—or to explore further.

"Penetrating so many secrets, we cease to believe in the unknowable. But there it sits nevertheless, calmly licking its chops."

H.L. Mencken, American essayist

Prologue

A Mystery for the Ages

In A.D. 114, Trajan, the *princeps*, or leader, of the Roman Empire, looked out across the waters of what is now called the Persian Gulf. He had just conquered the armies of Armenia, Assyria, and Mesopotamia. Trajan considered whether or not to push eastward as Alexander the Great, the famous Macedonian king, had five centuries before.

At one point, Alexander's army had refused to continue further eastward. Trajan knew his troops would offer no such resistance. They were Romans. They would go where their leader told them to. Still, Trajan was unsure about pressing onward. The Roman leader was sixty-three years old. He worried that he was too old to begin a new campaign. "If only I were younger," he said quietly to a nearby aide. Laying his reins against his horse's neck, Trajan turned back toward Rome.

Although he went no further, Trajan had already pushed the borders of the Roman Empire to their greatest extent. The empire included all the territory that bordered the Mediterranean Sea, from the point where Trajan stood in Asia Minor in the east to the Atlantic coast of present-day Spain in the west. It stretched from northern Africa in the south to northern Britain in the north. The area under Roman rule

included parts of more than thirty modern nations. It contained more than 100 million people. It was the largest empire the world had ever seen.

It also was the best organized. The areas conquered by Roman armies became part of a huge political system linked to Rome by law, trade, social customs, and fine stone roads. The people in conquered towns and cities were encouraged to elect or appoint their local leaders. Larger areas, known as provinces, were ruled by Roman governors. The governors reported to a group of elected officials known as the Roman Senate. The Senate, in turn, followed the leadership of the princeps or "first citizen."

The governors oversaw the day-to-day affairs of the state: the collection of taxes, the administration of justice, and the construction of public buildings. Everyone in the empire paid taxes to Rome, using coins that bore Roman inscriptions. They all were subject to the protection and penalties of Roman law.

Roman rule had brought peace and order to areas that had known only turmoil and bloodshed for centuries. Its armies were the most disciplined and powerful on earth. It seemed that the Roman Empire would last forever.

A Divided Empire

It did not. Within two hundred years of Trajan's death, the emperor Diocletian divided the vast empire into two parts. A few years later, in A.D. 323, the emperor Constantine moved the capital from Rome to the Turkish city of Byzantium, which was renamed Constantinople. Less than one hundred years later, Alaric the Goth led the members of his tribe to the outskirts of Rome. The once-proud Roman army was unable to stop the attack of the barbarians. Alaric and his forces sacked the city in 410.

Over the next fifty years, Rome was sacked several more times. Finally, in 476, a German military leader named Odoacer overthrew the emperor of the western Roman Empire, Romulus Augustulus.

The Via Appia, or the Appian Way, is one of the many fine roads the Romans built to help keep their empire united.

Odoacer pledged allegiance to the new emperor, Nepo, but the German tribesman in fact controlled the armies of Italy. The emperor had no real power. Nine hundred years of Roman self-rule had come to an end.

How did it happen? How could such a large and well-organized government be overcome by a nomadic tribe of barbarians? Historians have struggled to answer these questions for centuries. Many theories have been advanced. This book will explore this great historical mystery.

The Roman tax collectors were a common, if unwelcome, sight throughout the empire. The Romans spent public funds on roads, aqueducts, and public buildings that enhanced the lives of those who lived within the empire's borders.

One

What Was the Roman Empire?

The Roman Empire took its name from its capital, Rome, a city located on the Tiber River near the western coast of Italy. The founding of the city is steeped in legend. According to stories handed down for generations, it was founded by Romulus, the son of a princess from the city of Alba Longa. His mother was a descendant of Aeneas, a soldier from the ancient city of Troy who had founded Alba Longa after the Trojan War. The father of Romulus was said to be Mars, the god of war.

A Legendary Beginning

Legend says that Romulus' grandfather was overthrown by force. The wrongful king ordered Romulus and his twin brother Remus killed at birth. The man charged with carrying out the deed did not slay the young princes, however. Instead, he abandoned them near the Tiber River. Soon afterward, a she-wolf happened upon the infants. The wild creature kept the human children alive, warming them with her body and feeding them with her milk. A shepherd later discovered the two boys and raised them as his own.

When they were grown, Romulus and Remus led a rebellion against the king who had tried to kill them. They defeated his forces and restored their

(Opposite page) A Roman family at home. Many Roman men and women could read and write. They left behind a detailed record of daily life. Historians have searched through these writings for clues about the empire's demise.

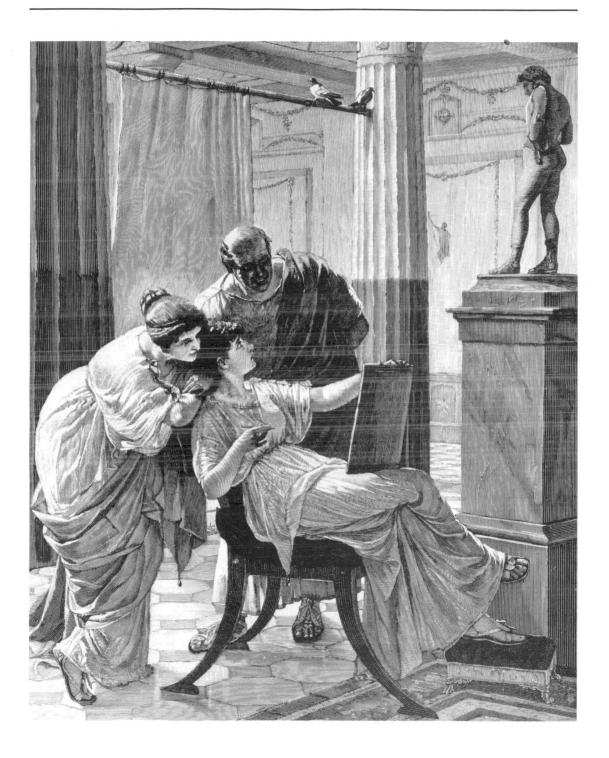

This famous sculpture depicts the story of Romulus and Remus who, according to legend, were nursed and warmed by a she-wolf.

grandfather to the throne of Alba Longa in 753 B.C. The young men then struck out on their own. Each decided to found a city along the banks of the Tiber. Romulus settled on a hill known as the Palatine Hill. Remus chose a hill known as the Aventine Hill.

The two new villages grew. Soon Romulus began to build a wall around his city. Watching as Romulus' workers laid down one row of bricks after another, Remus grew angry. He envied Romulus' design and wondered what his brother might be planning. To mock his brother's efforts, Remus charged toward the wall and vaulted over it. Enraged, Romulus killed Remus. "So will die whoever else shall leap over my walls," Romulus declared. For centuries, the Romans believed these bold words made their city immune to foreign attack.

Most of the people who had helped Romulus build his city were men. This presented a problem for Romulus. For his city to grow, he needed women to marry his settlers and bear children. According to the legends about the early history of Rome, Romulus devised a nasty scheme to bring women into the city. He challenged the Sabines, an ancient people who lived in the Apennine Mountains northeast of Rome, to compete in an athletic contest in Rome. The Sabines accepted. On the day of the contest, hundreds of Sabine men and women entered the new city. In the middle of the games, Romulus gave a secret signal to his followers. Instantly, some of the Roman men seized the Sabine women. The others attacked the Sabine men and drove them from the city. This event, known as the Rape of the Sabines, has been depicted in paintings and sculptures throughout history.

Chosen by Gods

According to legend, Romulus did not die, but rose into heaven. As he did so, he called for his city

According to legend, Romulus lured the Sabines into his new city and then took the Sabine women captive. This event, known as the Rape of the Sabines, has been depicted by many artists.

Rome's second king, Nusma Pompilus, enjoyed one of the longest and most peaceful reigns of any Roman leader. He also shaped the spiritual beliefs of the Roman people.

to become the capital of the world. Later, the Romans made much of this story. They believed their city was chosen by the gods to become the mightiest political power on earth. Eventually, it did.

A Religious Vision

Romulus was succeeded as Rome's king by a Sabine leader, Nusma Pompilus. He ruled over the city for forty-three peaceful years. During this time, he built a temple to the god Janus. He also claimed to have nightly meetings with a goddess named Egeria. Nusma Pompilus told the people of Rome that Egeria was teaching him the proper way to honor the gods—the rites to perform, prayers to say, songs to sing. At Egeria's direction, Nusma Pompilus built a temple to the goddess Vesta and introduced the people to the household gods Lares and Penates. These gods remained part of Roman life for a thousand years.

After Nusma Pompilus died, Tullus Hostilius ruled Rome. He led the Romans in a war against the people of Alba Longa. The Romans won the war and destroyed Alba Longa. This left Rome the most powerful city in the region.

Ancus Martius, the next king, greatly increased the city's size. He built a bridge across the Tiber, extending the city to Janiculum Hill. He also connected the city to the mouth of the Tiber, where the river met the Mediterranean Sea.

The Etruscans

The next three kings of Rome were Etruscans, a people who had settled in northern Italy. Little is known about the Etruscans. Historians are not certain where they came from or even what language they spoke. It is clear from the artifacts they left behind, however, that the Etruscans were skilled metal workers. They also must have traded with the Greeks, because the alphabet that the Etruscans passed on to the Romans was based on the Greek alphabet. Later, when the Romans conquered Europe, they took this alphabet with them. It was adopted by the people of Europe and handed down through the centuries. The words in this book are formed with letters derived from this alphabet.

The Etruscans also knew how to rule a large area. After they had conquered a city, they kept it under their control by appointing an Etruscan leader to govern it. The leaders of the conquered cities all kept in contact with each other. In times of crisis, such as famine or war, they called upon each other for aid. In this way, the Etruscans formed a league of cities in northern Italy loyal to the Etruscan king.

As this bronze sculpture shows, the Etruscans were skilled metal workers. The pose of the statue reflects the influence of Greek sculpture. It is just one of countless examples of how the Romans inherited Greek culture from the Etruscans.

In the seventh century B.C., the Etruscans conquered Rome. This was not all bad for the Romans. The Etruscans shared not only their alphabet but also their entire culture with the people of Rome. They taught the Romans their metal-working techniques. They passed along their love of Greek art, and they introduced the Romans to their gods, which they had taken from the Greeks.

An Orderly City

The Etruscans also taught the Romans how to make their city more orderly and prosperous. They set aside an area for public meetings, based on the Greek model of the open-air agora, where citizens could meet to discuss their problems. The site they chose became known as the Forum. The Etruscans taught the Romans important architectural techniques: how to construct the arch and the vault. These techniques allowed the Romans to build taller buildings, making it possible for more people to live in the city. At the height of the Roman Empire, it was common for people to live in apartment buildings several stories high.

Modeled after the Greek agora, the Roman Forum was a place for the citizens of Rome to discuss the issues of the day.

The Arch of Titus is just one example of the Roman builders' use of the arch, a building design brought to Rome by the Etruscans.

The Etruscans also passed along a number of customs that remained an important part of Roman life for centuries to come. The toga, the white woolen robe worn by Romans throughout the empire, came from the Etruscans. So did the fasces, the ax surrounded by a bundle of rods that was a symbol of the Roman leader's power.

The Etruscans brought the Romans into contact with other cities in the Etruscan realm and even beyond. Trade with the Greeks and other seafaring peoples became common. The Romans became part of the Mediterranean world—a world they would one day rule.

Three Etruscan kings ruled Rome. The last of these, Tarquin the Proud, was a cruel leader. In 509 B.C., a Roman citizen named Brutus roused the people of Rome to revolt against Tarquin. The Romans drove the Etruscan king from their city.

The Founding of the Republic

Brutus and his followers then made one of the most important political decisions in world history. They agreed that Rome would have no more kings. Instead, the people would choose two leaders from among themselves. These leaders, known as consuls, would rule for only one year each. This arrangement, the people reasoned, would prevent any one person from gaining too much power or ruling for too long. The form of government created by Brutus and his followers came to be known as a republic.

The two consuls shared power not only with each other, but also with a council of elders known as the Roman Senate. The Senate had been created under the Etruscan kings, but the Romans decided to keep it intact even after the Etruscans had been overthrown. Its members served for life. Although the Senate could not make laws, its advice was taken seriously by the consuls. After all, the consuls changed every year, but the Senate did not.

Under the new government, Romans began to feel that they were working together for the benefit of all, rather than for the good of a single person. Although only the wealthy could belong to the Senate or become a consul, most Romans believed the Senate and consuls acted in the interests of all the people. The Romans described this union in a single phrase: *senatus populusque Romans*, "the Roman senate and the people."

A Rising Power

As their city grew in size and wealth, the Romans began to trade with other cities and lands. Through trade, the Romans formed bonds with other

Italian cities. These ties led Rome to come to the aid of other cities when they were under attack. Beginning in 343 B.C., the Romans fought three wars on the soil of Italy. These wars, known as the Samnite Wars, left Rome in control of southern Italy.

During these conflicts, the Romans used a fighting formation known as a phalanx. The phalanx consisted of three lines of foot soldiers. Fighting in this formation required teamwork and discipline, but it was very effective. After fighting against Rome in the Samnite wars, a Greek king named Pyrrhus declared, "How easy it would be for me to conquer the world if I had Romans as my soldiers." Pyrrhus was astute. Within two hundred years, Roman soldiers would make their leaders the masters of the known world.

The Roman Senate was a council made up of the most wealthy and powerful elders of Rome.

The Roman conquest of the Mediterranean began in 246 B.C., when Rome began to battle the north African city of Carthage for control of Sicily, the great triangular island that lay between the two cities. These wars, known as the Punic Wars, were costly for both sides. Hundreds of thousands of soldiers died in battle. The Romans learned a great deal from these conflicts, however. They learned how to fight at sea. They also discovered how to plan large-scale military operations.

Hannibal

For example, during the Second Punic War in 218 B.C., the Carthaginian general Hannibal surprised the Romans by marching his troops more than one thousand miles from Spain, over the Alps into northern Italy. This feat was remarkable, especially since Hannibal's forces included a number of war elephants. Hannibal's army crushed the Roman resistance at Trebia in northern Italy. They also destroyed Roman forces at Lake Trasimene and Cannae. Forty thousand Roman troops died at Cannae

The Carthaginian general Hannibal surprised and terrified the Roman forces when he marched his war elephants from Spain, over the Alps, and into Italy during the Second Punic War.

Scipio Africanus led the attack on Carthage during the Second Punic War. His defeat of Hannibal on the plains of Zama opened the way for Roman domination of the Mediterranean.

alone. The Romans responded to these losses with a complex but effective plan.

An army under the command of the Roman general Fabius struck at Hannibal's forces in a series of skirmishes designed not to defeat Hannibal, but to slow the Carthaginian general's march toward Rome. From these efforts, the Roman general earned the nickname *Cunctator*, meaning "The Delayer." Meanwhile, a second Roman army prevented reinforcements from reaching Hannibal's army. Finally, the Roman general Scipio Africanus attacked Carthage itself. Seeing the Romans encamped on African soil, the leaders of Carthage sent word to Italy for Hannibal to return.

The great Carthaginian general arrived in Africa in time to engage the Roman forces on the plains of Zama. The fighting was fierce, bloody, and chaotic, but Roman discipline and weaponry prevailed. Hannibal's forces were defeated.

Sixty years later, the Romans fought the Third Punic War. The grandson of Scipio Africanus, Scipio Aemilianus, defeated the Carthaginians and destroyed their city. He ordered his troops not only to

At the end of the Third Punic War, the Roman forces completely destroyed the city of Carthage.

tear down the city's buildings, but actually to bury the rubble with plows. It is said that as he surveyed the barren site upon which the city had stood, Scipio wept. Turning to his friend Polybius, the Roman general said, "I fear and foresee that someday someone will give the same order about my fatherland." He was right, but the day he foresaw was nearly seven hundred years away.

The Making of the Empire

With Carthage defeated, Rome controlled the western Mediterranean. Scipio Aemilianus then marched his troops into Spain. After years of battle, the Romans were able to subdue the Spanish tribes. With the strongest army in the region, the Romans turned eastward. They soon made Dalmatia, Macedonia, and Greece their provinces.

In 59 B.C., the Roman leader Julius Caesar led Roman troops northward into Gaul—present-day France, Germany, Belgium, and northern Italy. After ten years of warfare, Caesar had conquered the bulk of Europe. He then led his forces eastward into Asia Minor. After defeating the forces he met, Caesar summarized his exploits in a three-word phrase that has lived through the ages, *"Veni, vidi, vici,"* Latin for "I came, I saw, I conquered."

Caesar's successor, Octavian, also known as Caesar Augustus, extended Roman rule into Syria, Judea, and Egypt. By the time of the birth of Christ, Roman provinces encircled the Mediterranean, which the Romans began to refer to as *mare nostrum*—"our sea." Less than one hundred years later, Trajan became the ruler of Rome and pushed the borders of the empire to their greatest extent. The Romans ruled the entire known world.

Julius Caesar brought much of present-day Europe under Roman control. His account of this campaign, *The Gallic Wars*, survived the fall of Rome and is still read today.

Two

The Decline of Rome

(Opposite page) In this picture, Constantine directs a stone cutter to engrave "Constantinople" onto a pillar in the city of Byzantium. Actually, the emperor renamed the city "New Rome," but everyone called it Constantinople, or "Constantine's city."

"In the second century of the Christian era, the Empire of Rome comprehended the fairest part of the earth, and the most civilized portion of mankind," wrote the British historian Edward Gibbon in his six-volume history, *The Decline and Fall of the Roman Empire*, the first volume of which was published in 1776. For Gibbon, human civilization reached its peak under Roman rule from A.D. 96 to 180. He wrote:

> If a man were called to fix the period in the history of the world during which the condition of the human race was most happy and prosperous, he would without hesitation, name that which elapsed from the death of Domitian to the accession of Commodus. . . .

The frontiers of that extensive monarchy were guarded by ancient renown and disciplined valor. The gentle but powerful influence of laws and manners had gradually cemented the union of provinces. Their peaceful inhabitants enjoyed and abused the advantages of luxury. The image of a free constitution was preserved with decent reverence: the Roman senate appeared to possess the sovereign authority, and devolved upon the emperors all the executive powers of government. During a happy period [A.D. 96-

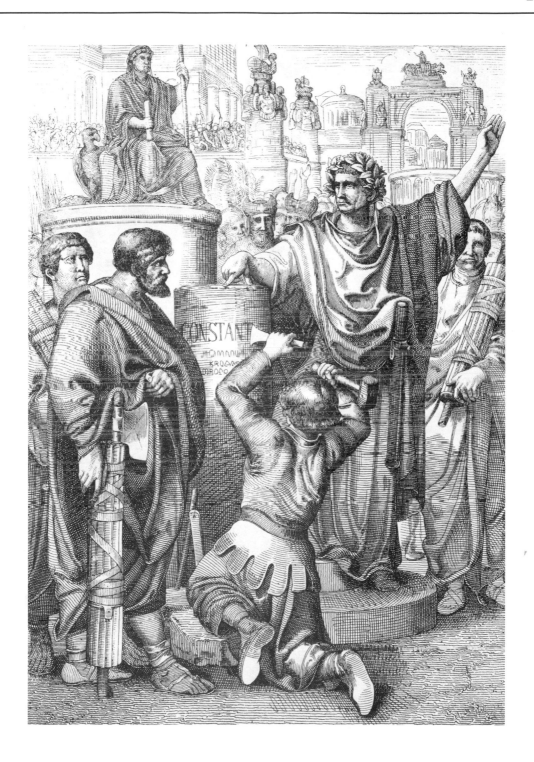

A statue depicts Marcus Aurelius, the last of the "Five Good Emperors."

"The two greatest problems in history are how to account for the rise of Rome, and how to account for her fall."

J.S. Reid, *Cambridge Medieval History*

"The decline of Rome was the natural and inevitable effect of immoderate greatness."

Edward Gibbon, *The Decline and Fall of the Roman Empire*, 1776

180] of more than fourscore years, the public administration was conducted by the virtue and abilities of Nerva, Trajan, Hadrian, and the two Antonines.

The period of social harmony Gibbon described is often referred to as the *Pax Romana*, or "Roman Peace." From this summit of civil achievement, Gibbon believed, the Romans began a slow descent into the valley of social decay. Discipline and manners gave way to luxury and the pursuit of pleasure. Some Roman leaders began to ignore the existing laws, replacing them with decrees based on their own whims and desires. Others tried to restore the rule of law and lead the people back toward the heights of Roman glory. Most, however, followed the easy path downward. Finally, the once-proud empire lay in ruins.

The trouble began with Marcus Aurelius. A brilliant general and strong leader, Marcus Aurelius was the last of the "Five Good Emperors" that Gibbon admired. His mistake came not in how he ruled but in whom he chose as his successor. That person was his son, Commodus. When Commodus was just fifteen, Marcus Aurelius made him co-emperor. Four years later, Marcus Aurelius died, and his son took over.

Although raised to lead, Commodus possessed few virtues and little common sense. He murdered thousands of people he believed were his enemies. He enriched himself without doing anything to enhance the empire. His harsh rule caused the people to lose confidence in their leaders and their government. Finally, after thirteen years, Commodus was murdered in A.D. 193.

The Year of Four Emperors

Commodus was not the first corrupt leader Rome had known, but his evil lived on in an especially harmful way. He had transformed an elite corps of Roman soldiers known as the Praetorian Guard into a band of brutal thugs. These powerful soldiers did not respect the man who succeeded

Augustus formed the Praetorian Guard to protect the emperor. The elite corps became so powerful in the second century that it deposed some emperors and chose others.

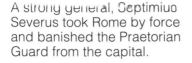

A strong general, Septimius Severus took Rome by force and banished the Praetorian Guard from the capital.

Commodus, a leader named Pertinax. After just eighty-six days, the Praetorians murdered the new princeps. They placed Pertinax's severed head on a spear and offered their loyalty to the person who would pay them the most for it. A wealthy senator named Julian stepped forward. True to their word, the Praetorians made Julian the leader of the empire.

Julian's reign was short, however. Within sixty-six days, a Roman general named Septimius Severus marched his legions into Rome and took the throne by force. He executed Julian and banished the Praetorian Guard from Rome.

Severus soon restored the government's prestige and power. He repeated Marcus Aurelius' mistake, however, by leaving the empire to a son who had neither the temperament nor the wisdom to lead. The first act of this young man, Caracalla, was to murder his younger brother, Geta, with whom he had shared power. For the next six years, Caracalla traveled throughout the provinces, killing, raping, and plundering at will.

News of Caracalla's misdeeds spread throughout the Roman world. The fabric of Roman life, already weakened by the reign of Commodus and the turmoil of the Year of Four Emperors, began to unravel under Caracalla's brutal hands. Finally, in 217, Caracalla was assassinated.

The plot that ended Caracalla's life was but one of many forces tugging on the strands that held the empire together. For the next seventy years, well-armed generals and powerful senators vied for the leadership of Rome. Some ruled for only a few months. Others were even less fortunate. Their reigns lasted weeks or even days. Meanwhile, one province after another tore away from Roman rule.

Dividing the Empire

One of the few Roman leaders to make any progress toward mending the tattered empire was Diocletian, who ruled from 284 to 305. Believing the empire too large to be governed by one person, Diocletian divided it into two parts—an eastern half

Diocletian split the Roman Empire into two parts, the eastern half and the western half.

and western half. The ruler of each half held the title of *augustus*. Each augustus, in turn, appointed a *caesar* to assist him. This system became known as a tetrarchy, meaning "rule by four leaders."

At first, Diocletian's plan helped hold the empire together, but later the two halves drifted apart. After Diocletian retired, war broke out among the four members of the tetrarchy. The son of one of these rulers, Constantine, marched on Rome in 312 and defeated his rival, Maxentius. Constantine made himself Emperor of the West. Eleven years later, he attacked and defeated the Emperor of the East, uniting the empire under his rule. Constantine then moved the capital of the empire to the ancient Turkish city of Byzantium (now Istanbul), naming the city New

Constantinople (now Istanbul) served as the capital of the eastern half of the Roman Empire for eleven centuries.

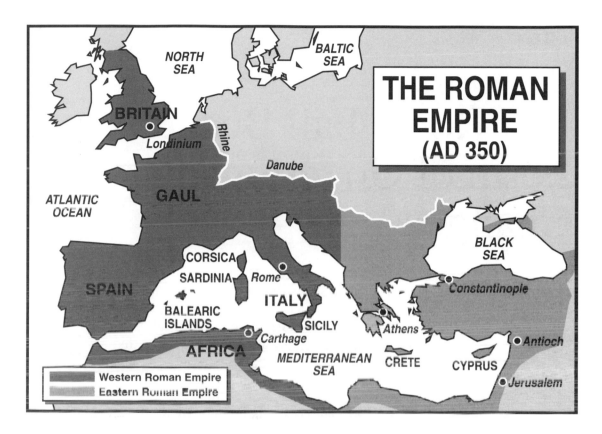

THE ROMAN EMPIRE (AD 350)

- Western Roman Empire
- Eastern Roman Empire

Rome, but everyone called it Constantinople, or "Constantine's city." While Constantine lived, he ruled over a single, vast state, but his decision to move the capital from Rome further divided the empire.

A Fallen Empire

For nearly sixty years, Roman emperors ruled from Constantine's great city. The last of these, Theodosius, again divided the empire into East and West, leaving one half to each of his sons. Fifteen years later, a northern European tribesman named Alaric the Goth led a successful raid on Rome. Not long afterward, the western half of the empire fell into the hands of the raiding barbarians. The once-mighty empire had fallen.

Three

Did Rome Fall Because Its Form of Government Changed?

When the Romans built their empire, they lived under one type of government. When they lost it, they lived under another. Did the change in Roman government cause the empire to fall? Some historians, including Edward Gibbon, believe that it did. Others are not so sure. Perhaps other factors—disease, changing moral values, or the strength of invading tribes—were more important than the changes in Roman government, they argue. In fact, some historians, including Richard Mansfield Haywood, author of *The Myth of Rome's Fall*, believe that the changes in Roman government strengthened the Roman state and prolonged the life of the empire.

To understand the debate about Roman government, one must examine the form of government under which the Romans lived as they began to build their empire, then trace how that government changed over the next several centuries.

The Roman Republic

The great Roman expansion occurred in a two-hundred-year period right before the birth of Christ. At this time, the Roman Republic was at its height. The government was similar to, though not exactly the same as, the government formed after the Etruscan kings were driven from Rome in 509 B.C.

(Opposite page) In the Roman Republic, the Senate decided the most important business of the state. Later, this power shifted to the emperors. Did this change cause the empire to fall?

The wealthiest and most powerful Romans, the patricians, wore togas made of the finest materials.

At first, all members of the Senate belonged to the upper class of Romans, known as patricians. Members of the patrician class were very wealthy. Most owned large tracts of land. They had the greatest knowledge of the law, and they used it to their advantage. Many also provided military leadership.

Even patricians who were not members of the Senate had a great deal of influence in affairs of the state. Some were members of the *comitia centuriata*, an assembly of advisors created by the second Etruscan king, Servius Tullius. Like the Senate, the comitia centuriata was preserved by the Romans after the formation of the republic.

Romans who were not members of the patrician class were known as plebeians. Most plebeians were poor, but many were members of the middle class. A few plebeians—mostly merchants—were wealthy.

Plebeians were welcome to serve in the Roman army. They even could be elected to the comitia centuriata. Their voice in assembly was not great, however, since the votes of the patricians counted more than the votes of plebeians.

The Struggle of Orders

Unhappy with their lack of power, the plebeians decided to leave Rome in 499 B.C. and form their own city. This action was known as the First Secession. Rather than lose so many hardworking citizens, the consuls and the Senate offered the plebeians a deal. They created a new official, the tribune. This office would be filled by a plebeian. At first there were two tribunes; later the number grew to five. The tribune had the power to veto, or stop, any action taken by the consuls or the Senate.

Over the next 120 years, the plebeians pressed for even greater reforms in Roman government. Wishing to maintain their power, the patricians resisted these efforts. The conflict between the plebeians and the patricians became known as the Struggle of Orders.

Step by step, the plebeians prevailed in their efforts to gain more power. In 471 B.C., they were allowed to form their own governing body, the *concilium plebis*. Through this assembly, the plebeians were able to enact laws regarding their own welfare. In 445 B.C., plebeians were allowed for the first time to marry patricians. In 376 B.C., the Senate passed a law that required that one of Rome's two consuls be a plebeian. Soon afterward, wealthy plebeians were permitted to gain seats in the Senate. Finally, in 287 B.C., a law known as *lex Hortensia* was enacted. This measure stated that laws passed by the concilium plebis were binding on all citizens, plebeian and patrician alike.

The struggle for civil power was difficult, yet the Romans had never let their disagreements get out of hand. They did not, for example, ever war among themselves. As a result, the people of Rome emerged from the Struggle of Orders with a strong sense of unity.

Chances for Advancement

Some historians believe this unity played a decisive role in Rome's future conquests. The soldiers who marched under the Roman standard were not risking their lives to enrich a distant monarch. In many ways, they were fighting for themselves. Each veteran of the Roman army was given a parcel of land after he retired. If a soldier was not a Roman citizen, his military service could earn him citizenship. With citizenship came the protection of Roman law and the right to run for civil offices. In theory, any Roman citizen could aspire to be the leader of Rome.

The sense of participation was even stronger for officers in the Roman army. Successful generals often were elected to the Senate or the office of consul. Under a king or queen, an officer might look forward to gaining a few spoils of war, but his position in life would not really change. In the Roman Republic, an officer who served with distinction could advance through the ranks of the army and attain a position in the Roman government. The lure of civil power inspired many Roman officers to act wisely and fight bravely in the field.

The Romans were very proud of their republic, and they guarded it fiercely. They hated the word "king," and they were willing to do whatever was necessary to keep their republic from becoming a monarchy. With the most powerful army on earth, the Romans had little to fear from distant kings and queens. A powerful Roman leader, however, was a different story. The Romans were constantly on guard that none of their consuls or generals should make themselves king.

Despite their fears of being ruled by a king, the Romans were willing from time to time to give

"The masters of the Roman world surrounded their throne with darkness, concealed their irresistible strength, and humbly professed themselves the accountable ministers of the senate."

Edward Gibbon, *The Decline and Fall of the Roman Empire*, 1776

"Augustus sought new solutions to the problems confronting Rome. The result was a system of government capable of administering an empire with justice and fairness."

John P. McKay, Bennett D. Hill, John Buckler, *A History of Western Society*, 1987

nearly total power to one person. Times of crisis, the Romans believed, required the strong leadership of a single person. They called such a leader a *magister populi*, or dictator. The dictator was chosen by the two consuls, acting with the support of the Senate. The dictator was allowed to appoint an assistant known as the *magister equitum*, or "master of the horse." The dictator and the master of the horse held their powers for a maximum of six months.

The ideal Roman dictator was Cincinnatus, a patrician known throughout the republic for his leadership skills. The Senate named Cincinnatus dictator when a mountain tribe known as the Aequi threatened Rome in 458 B.C. Cincinnatus left his farm, assumed control of the Roman army, and attacked the Aequi. The war was brief. After just sixteen days, the Aequi retreated, and Cincinnatus returned to Rome in triumph. With the army under his

A Roman officer encourages his troops. Successful military leaders were often rewarded with powerful positions in the civil government.

control and the people in his debt, Cincinnatus could have proclaimed himself king, but he did not. Instead, he immediately resigned his dictatorship and returned to his estate.

A later Roman dictator, Julius Caesar, was not so willing to give up his power. Perhaps the strongest leader in Western history, Caesar became consul in 59 B.C. He shared power with two other consuls, Crassus and Pompey, in what later became known as the First Triumvirate, or rule of three. Crassus, the eldest of the three men, ruled over the eastern part of the empire. Pompey governed Rome itself, Italy, Spain, and North Africa. Caesar ruled over the northern portion of the empire, known as Gaul, for ten years.

Dictator for Life

During this time, Julius Caesar pushed the Roman frontier further north than ever before, into present-day France, Germany, and Great Britain. His account of these campaigns, entitled *Gallic Wars*, has survived to modern times. It is one of the best sources of information about the Roman army of this period. Because of Caesar's success in Gaul, Roman arts, letters, law, and values became a permanent part of European culture.

In 53 B.C., the army of Crassus was defeated by the Parthians in Asia Minor. Crassus was murdered as he tried to discuss the terms of peace. With Crassus dead, Caesar worried that Pompey would gain control of the rest of the empire. Caesar decided to act quickly, before Pompey had time to consolidate his power. Caesar marched his troops south across the Rubicon River and into Italy. Once he had taken this step, Caesar had no choice but to defeat Pompey or to die trying. If he retreated or surrendered, he would be killed for treason. Ever since Caesar's time, the phrase "crossing the Rubicon" has been used to describe an important action that cannot be undone.

Pompey served as a consul in the First Triumvirate. Later, he was driven from Italy by Julius Caesar.

Caesar prevailed. Pompey surrendered Italy without a fight, choosing to make his stand in Greece instead. Caesar had the Senate name him as dictator, then he and his army followed Pompey across the Adriatic Sea. The two armies met near the city of Pharsalia. Caesar's forces triumphed, and Pompey fled to Egypt. Caesar pursued Pompey to the shores of North Africa. Fearing Caesar, the Egyptians murdered Pompey and offered his embalmed head as a gift of peace to the new Roman conqueror. It is said that Caesar wept with sorrow when he saw his one-time partner's severed head.

Julius Caesar leads his troops across the Rubicon River, knowing he must succeed in his campaign against Pompey or face certain death.

In Egypt, Caesar joined forces with an Egyptian princess named Cleopatra against her rivals for the throne of Egypt. Again successful, Caesar returned to Rome with Cleopatra as his lover and ally. Caesar asked the Senate to proclaim him "Dictator for Life." The council could hardly oppose the wishes of the conqueror, and Caesar officially became the most powerful man in the world.

Striking a Blow for the Republic

Caesar's enemies were unhappy with Caesar's conduct, and even some of his friends were troubled by his actions. They worried that he might marry Cleopatra and try to pass the empire on to his heir, as a king would. A number of senators met in secret to discuss the matter. They decided that Caesar did indeed intend to make himself king. To preserve the

Julius Caesar backed Cleopatra in her bid to become queen of Egypt, and the two leaders became lovers. Rumors about their possible marriage heightened fears that Caesar planned to make himself king.

republic, they agreed, Caesar must die. They took a pledge to assassinate the dictator when he appeared before the Senate. Each of the conspirators promised to carry a dagger, so that no one person or group could be blamed for the murder. They would kill, they believed, for the good of the Roman people.

On the Ides of March (March 15), 44 B.C., twenty-three Roman senators attacked Julius Caesar. One by one, the men thrust their daggers into the body of the Dictator for Life. Their actions did not keep Rome from falling into the hands of a king, however. In a sense, they hastened it.

Augustus

Upon hearing the news of Caesar's death, the dictator's great-nephew, Octavian, came to Rome to take charge of the government. With the help of Caesar's friend, a general named Mark Antony, Octavian defeated the armies loyal to Caesar's killers. Octavian then fought Mark Antony for control of the empire, after Antony had allied himself with

On the Ides of March in 44 B.C., twenty-three Roman senators attacked and killed Julius Caesar. Though Caesar's murder was meant to preserve the Roman Republic, it had the opposite effect.

Cleopatra joined forces with Mark Antony to battle Octavian on the sea near Actium, Greece.

Cleopatra. Victorious over Antony and Cleopatra's forces in a sea battle near Actium, Greece, Octavian returned to Rome in triumph. The parade celebrating his victory lasted three days. The new Roman leader promised to restore the republic, but in fact he did not. Instead, he became its first monarch.

How did Octavian manage to make himself king among a people who hated the very word? The answer is simple. He avoided the word while accepting every power the word implied. The title he chose for himself was not king, but *princeps*, or "first citizen." With this modest title came powers unknown by any of Rome's earlier leaders. Grateful that Octavian had brought peace to the empire after years of civil war, the Senate declared that he would be reelected consul every year for the rest of his life. The Senate also made Octavian proconsul, or ruler over all the armies of all the provinces. With this power, no person in the empire could challenge Octavian's power. He was dictator in fact, if not in name.

The Senate also conferred upon Octavian the title *augustus*, meaning "exalted." In the eastern empire, the newly named Augustus (Octavian) was declared a god. Soon, everyone in the empire was expected to pay homage to Augustus as a deity—another first for a Roman leader.

Though vast, these powers themselves did not make Augustus a king or emperor. What made him

Octavian became known as Caesar Augustus, the "exalted Caesar." Although he referred to himself merely as "First Citizen," Augustus was in fact Rome's first emperor.

a monarch was the manner in which his successor was chosen. In a monarchy, succession is determined by birth: The crown is passed from parents to their children or to other close relations. That is what happened under Augustus.

Before he died, Augustus informed the Senate that he wished for his stepson, Tiberius, to succeed him as princeps. The Senate agreed to this arrangement. Since control of the empire was determined by birth rather than by election, even Augustus' staunchest defenders had to admit that the great Roman leader had created a monarchy. The Roman Republic had come to an end.

The Principate

Few Romans protested the change. Thirty years had passed since Julius Caesar had been killed to preserve the republic. During those years, Augustus had brought peace and prosperity to the entire Mediter-

Tiberius was chosen by his stepfather, Augustus, to become the leader of the Roman Empire, leaving no doubt that the Roman Republic had been replaced by a monarchy.

ranean area. Rome had grown rich. Augustus had used wealth collected from the provinces to build great stadiums, temples, and public buildings. It was said that Augustus had "found Rome built of sundried brick and left it clothed in marble." Life under a princeps had been good. Most Romans wished for it to continue.

The first Roman monarchs also took care to preserve the illusion of the republic. Augustus gave the Senate command of the most peaceful provinces—Greece, Crete, Sicily, Sardinia, Spain, Syria, Cyrene, Bithynia, Asia Minor, and North Africa. He allowed the concilium plebis to continue enacting laws and electing consuls. Neither he, Tiberius, nor any of their immediate successors named themselves king. The illusion of the republican government lived on.

One thing a monarchy often offers to a society is a peaceful transfer of power from one leader to the next. At first, this was true of the new Roman monarchy as well. For nearly one hundred years, the throne of Rome passed peacefully from one relation to another. Tiberius (A.D. 14-37) was succeeded by Caligula (37-41), Claudius (41-54), and Nero (54-68), all of whom were related to Augustus. After the death of Nero, however, civil war broke out. The victor in this war, Vespasian, did not try to restore the republic. Indeed, he made no pretense that Rome was a republic at all. He made sure that his power was transferred directly to his sons Titus (79-81) and Domitian (81-96).

An Established Monarchy

Domitian ran the empire harshly, and he was assassinated. By this time, the monarchy was so well established that no one seriously considered returning to the system of being ruled by two consuls. Instead, the Senate made an elderly senator named Nerva the emperor. Realizing that he needed an heir, Nerva adopted a strong leader named Trajan as his son. The throne passed to Trajan in A.D. 98.

Vespasian took Rome by force when civil war broke out after Nero's death. Instead of restoring the republic, Vespasian strengthened the monarchy.

Nerva and Trajan were the first two of what have come to be known as the Five Good Emperors. All five of these men were related to each other, though not as fathers and sons. It was their years of rule that Edward Gibbon described as "the period in the history of the world during which the condition of the human race was most happy and prosperous." Had all the Roman emperors governed as wisely as these five did, there would be little reason to think that the change to a monarchy caused the empire to collapse. This was not the case, however.

A Flawed System

The last of the Five Good Emperors, Marcus Aurelius, left the throne to his selfish and cruel son, Commodus. According to those who believe that the change to a monarchy caused the collapse of the empire, Commodus's rise to the throne was not merely a sad accident of history. Such a painful turn of events was bound to occur, Gibbon and other historians contend, because the monarchical system is flawed. It contains no safeguards against the accession of an inept, enfeebled, or evil leader. When leadership is determined by birth alone, the happiness of millions is entrusted to the laws of genetic chance. Sooner or later, an heir to the throne will be born who is not equipped to govern. Such a leader can do great damage to an empire or a nation.

The Roman Empire had its share of weak, insane, and inept monarchs. Usually such leaders were murdered. These slayings rid the empire of bad leaders, but they often caused problems of their own. Sometimes the slain leader's family, friends, or military allies would avenge his death by killing the rival who replaced him. The vicious cycle would continue until an especially powerful leader emerged. In the meantime, the day-to-day affairs of the empire suffered. This sort of bloody turmoil reached its peak in the third century, but it continued into the fourth century as well. The waste of human life in these battles weakened the empire at the very moment that the invading tribes were growing stronger.

Had the Romans clung to their republican ideals, they might have avoided the wars of succession that occurred during the monarchy. After all, the term of the consul was very brief and the office promised few rewards. It is hard to imagine that a leader would risk war for such a meager prize. The emperor, on the other hand, ruled for life and enjoyed great riches. The grandeur of the imperial throne lured many of Rome's ablest leaders into bloody battles for its control.

The terms of office in the republic might have solved another problem that plagued the empire: prolonged rule by a poor or deranged leader. Consul terms were limited to just two years. Even the worst consul could not seriously damage the vast empire in such a short time.

The republican government had problems, too, however. In times of crisis, the Senate had to turn to a strong leader, or dictator, for guidance. Although a few dictators gladly gave up their powers when the crisis was resolved, others did not. This is not surprising. Strong leaders often crave power. They rarely want to see such power pass to those less capable than themselves.

"Monarchy was . . . an inescapable result of the existence of the empire; the more efficient the imperial government became the more it assumed new functions; and the more that increasing pressure made its task heavier, so much the more it became monarchical."

Mason Hammond, *The Antonine Monarchy*, 1959

"In [Nero's] history one discerns the outstanding weakness of a hereditary system; men with neither character nor experience can come to positions of absolute power."

Allan Massie, twentieth-century British historian

Four

Did Christianity Destroy the Empire?

When the Romans built their empire, they practiced one religion. When the empire collapsed, they practiced another. Just as some historians believe the change in Roman government caused the empire to fall, other historians believe the change in religious beliefs caused its decline. What were these changes? What effect, if any, did they have on the empire?

Roman Animism

The earliest Romans believed that unseen beings dwelled within nature. Every river, spring, lake, and tree was inhabited by a spirit, they believed. These spirits were the cause of natural events such as storms, lightning, wind, rainbows, floods, drought, disease, and healing. The belief that natural objects have spirits is known as animism, from the Latin word *anima*, meaning "soul."

The spirits revered by the early Romans did not have distinct personalities. Each was a shapeless entity known only by its unique power, or numen. The Romans regarded these spirits with awe and respect. They believed they had to ask permission of the spirits before taking anything from nature. For example, Romans left a small offering, such as food, before taking water from a lake or river. A sacrifice was required before a person could cut

down a tree. Unless a person performed the proper rite, Romans believed, something bad would happen to that person. For example, the water might make the drinker ill, or the woodcutter might get cut by his own ax.

The Coming of the Gods

Contact with the Greeks and Etruscans changed Roman religious beliefs. The Romans began to give their local spirits names and personalities. They started to refer to them as *dei*, or "gods." This practice is known as deism.

The Romans based their descriptions of the gods on Greek and Etruscan models. For example, river gods were said to look like strong men with the horns of an ox. The nymphs in charge of trees appeared as beautiful young women. The nymphs who ruled springs and fountains looked like women from the waist up. Below the waist, they had fishlike tails like their cousins in the oceans and the seas, the mermaids.

The Romans began to tell stories about their gods and goddesses. Within these stories, known as myths, Romans began to explore the relationship between human beings, the universe, and spiritual powers. Again they borrowed from the Greeks and Etruscans, adopting these people's tales about the world's creation and its mastery by divine beings. For example, the Romans adopted the Greek belief that the world was ruled by twelve mighty gods. The Romans gave these gods new names, but gave the same powers to them that the Greeks had. Jupiter was king of the gods and ruler of the heavens. Juno, his wife, was the queen of the gods. Neptune, Jupiter's brother, was the god of the sea and of horses. Ceres was the goddess of agriculture, marriage, and fertility. Vulcan was the god of fire and metallurgy. Minerva, the daughter of Jupiter, was the goddess of wisdom, war, the arts, and crafts. Mars was the god of war. Venus was the goddess of

A statue depicts Juno, the queen of the gods, whom the Romans adopted from the Greek goddess, Hera.

love and beauty. Apollo was the god of music, poetry, medicine, prophecy, archery, and young unmarried men. Diana was the goddess of hunting, the moon, and young unmarried women. Mercury served as the messenger of the gods and the god of science, commerce, travel, eloquence, and cunning. Vesta was the goddess of home and hearth.

The Romans worshipped Diana, depicted here driving a chariot, as the goddess of hunting, the moon, and young unmarried women.

A Host of Gods

In addition to the major gods, the Romans also began to worship many minor gods and goddesses. One of these was Faunus, god of forests, flocks, and shepherds. The son of Mercury, Faunus had the head and torso of a man and the legs, hooves, and tail of a goat. He also had small horns on his head and a little beard. When startled, he let out such an eerie, grating scream that any humans who happened to hear it were seized with sudden fear. The Greek name for this god was Pan. Today, we still call a sudden, overpowering fear "panic" in memory of this god.

Another minor god of importance to the Romans was Janus, god of windows and doors, beginnings and endings. It was after Janus that the Romans named the first month of the year *Januarius*, which we call January. Maia, goddess of spring, is another minor god whose name became part of the calendar. (Two other months, March and June, were named after major gods, Mars and Juno.)

As stated earlier, Nusma Pompilus, the second king of Rome, claimed to have nightly meetings with a nymph named Egeria. It was this spirit, Nusma said, who introduced him to the minor gods Lares and Penates, who ruled over the Roman household. The Romans also continued to pay homage to the countless local deities and spirits.

Restless Spirits

The Romans also believed that the spirits of the dead haunted certain places. To placate these restless spirits, the Romans left small gifts for the dead. The poet Ovid described this custom in his poem *Fasti:*

> The spirits of the dead ask for little.
> They are more grateful for piety than for an
> expensive gift—
> Not greedy are the gods who haunt the Styx
> below:
> A rooftile covered with a sacrificial crown,
> Scattered kernels, a few grains of salt,
> Bread dipped in wine, and loose violets—
> These are enough.
> Put them in a potsherd and leave them in the
> middle of the road.

From the beginning, Romans viewed their relationship with the divine as a practical matter. They made offerings to unseen spirits, and later to gods, to appease them and gain their favor. This is not to say the Romans did not feel genuine awe and respect toward the divine. They did. But they also believed that once they had shown their respect to the gods, they had fulfilled their duty. They did not believe anything more was required of them. The Roman religion was based on simple rituals, not on prolonged study, meditation, or prayer.

Unlike peoples who believed their gods were free to do as they pleased, the Romans believed their gods were bound to them by a sort of divine contract. Each person was expected to honor the

A Roman priest performs a ritual before a statue of Jupiter. The Romans believed that even the mightiest gods were bound to grant them favors, provided they performed the proper rituals.

gods, but the gods were expected to grant their worshipers their desired favors. If the god failed to hold up its end of the bargain, then it might be considered unworthy of further worship.

The Roman Priesthood

The Romans believed their offerings and sacrifices had a direct effect on their daily life, so they took great care to perform their rituals correctly. Roman priests enjoyed great social prestige because they alone knew the exact manner in which to perform the rituals. The priesthood was important for another reason as well. The Romans believed the gods ruled over community life, so the community was required to pay its respects to the gods. Priests performed this task on behalf of the group. They presided over public ceremonies to honor the gods. They declared holidays. They took care of the temples. They advised the leaders on the rituals to be performed when conducting public business.

Priests were also the keepers of religious law. They knew which human actions offended the gods, and how these crimes should be punished. In Roman society, religious law and secular law were entwined. As a result, the priests had to be consulted before legal affairs and state business could be settled.

The Roman priests belonged to a kind of guild known as the College of Priests. The college was headed by the *pontifex maximus*, who was elected by the people. He appointed the King of Priests, or *rex sacrorum*, to preside over public ceremonies. The title King of Priests harked back to the days before the founding of the republic. In those times, the king served as the chief priest. The rex sacrorum held the highest rank in the College of Priests, even though he was appointed by the pontifex maximus.

The people nominated to be priests did not come from a special religious order or class. They were chosen from among the leading citizens. Many magistrates, senators, and even consuls belonged to the College of Priests. Because religious law played a major role in state conduct, many powerful Romans took care to become priests. Julius Caesar, for example, not only became a priest, but served as pontifex maximus from 63 B.C. until his death in 44 B.C. While serving as dictator, Caesar enlarged the priesthood, nominating many of his friends and allies to the College of Priests.

Auspices and Auguries

The Romans believed that the gods revealed their will through natural, physical signs. For example, they believed the flight of birds could foretell events. Omens derived from the movement of birds were known as the auspices. The Romans also believed that the entrails of sacrificed animals held clues about the future. These signs were known as the auguries.

Certain priests, called augurs, were responsible for reading these signs. The augurs did not belong to the College of Priests, but to a separate priesthood, the College of Augurs. It was Roman custom to take the auspices or consult the auguries before making major decisions. If the augurs found a bad omen, they could suspend state action, or even reverse it.

As the Romans conquered the Mediterranean world, they took their beliefs with them. They expected the people they conquered to honor the Roman holidays and rituals. They did not, however, require conquered peoples to give up their own religious practices or beliefs. Since the Romans already believed in many gods, they had no reason to fear or hate new gods they encountered in foreign lands. Rome objected to local religions only if they caused people to be disloyal to the empire.

Because of the excellence and safety of Roman roads, and because the seas were free of pirates, ideas spread quickly through the Roman Empire. As a result, Romans learned about many new religions.

A Roman augur prepares to examine the entrails of a bird for signs and omens. This practice was known as taking the auguries.

Sometimes they adopted foreign beliefs as their own. For example, the Egyptian goddess Isis gained a large following among Romans. She was worshipped as the goddess of life, death, and love. Romans believed she could cure diseases, work miracles, and grant eternal life. Viewed as the ideal mother, wife, and lover, Isis was especially popular among Roman women.

The Romans influenced religious thought in the lands they conquered, as well. During the second century B.C., some Greeks began to worship the goddess Roma as the personification of the Roman state. In some Greek cities, people had long regarded their kings as gods. It was only natural for them to worship their Roman conquerors in the same way. Cults devoted to Julius Caesar, Mark Antony, and others arose among the Greeks.

The worship of kings was common in Asia as well. During the reign of Augustus, temples to Roma and Augustus began to appear in the eastern part of the empire. Augustus did not discourage such homage to himself. He knew that such worship strengthened the Roman hold on these conquered lands. The cult of Roma and Augustus spread to other parts of the empire as well. In 12 B.C., an altar to Roma and Augustus was built in Gaul, near the ancient city of Lugdunum (now Lyons, France). Another sprang up near present-day Cologne, Germany.

Augustus could not permit such worship to spread to Italy, however. If he agreed to be worshipped as a god, Augustus could hardly claim that his power came from the people, and that he was merely the first citizen, or princep. He did allow the people of Rome to pay homage to his guiding spirit, or *genius*, however. Between 12 and 7 B.C., 265 shrines were built to Lares and the Genius of Augustus—one shrine for each city precinct. In southern Italy, people began to worship the princep himself, not just his genius.

The Cult of the Living Emperors

Whether people prayed to the emperor or to his guiding spirit, such rituals helped unite the empire. For this reason, emperors who followed Augustus encouraged their own worship. The worship of Roman leaders became known as the Cult of the Living Emperors, or the Imperial Cult.

This engraving depicts Moses receiving the Ten Commandments from God. The First Commandment forbade the worship of any god other than the one known as Yahweh.

Not all of the people conquered by Rome were willing to accept Roman religious rituals or the Cult of the Living Emperors, no matter how public and superficial these customs may have been. The greatest resistance came in Judea. For thousands of years, the Jews had worshipped only one god, a practice known as monotheism. The laws that formed the foundation of Jewish culture, the Law of Moses, also known as the Ten Commandments, forbade the worship of any god other than the one known as Yahweh. Even the formal rituals honoring Roma and the living emperor violated these sacred laws, so the Jews refused to take part in the Roman custom. The Romans considered these views at best unreasonable and at worst treasonous.

Judaism

The religion of the Jews, Judaism, was much more than a spiritual faith. It was a legal system, political system, and way of life. The Romans recognized the importance of Judaism when Pompey annexed Judea as a province in 64 B.C. Instead of placing a governor in charge of the province, Pompey handpicked a Jewish high priest, knowing that he would serve as the head of government as well. In 37 B.C., the Romans installed Herod, who was loyal to Rome, as the king of Judea. Herod ruled wisely and rebuilt the temple of Jerusalem, earning himself the nickname Herod the Great. Although they paid taxes to Rome, the Jews enjoyed limited self-rule until A.D. 6, when Augustus overthrew Herod's successor, Archelaus, and placed Judea under the rule of a Roman prefect, a type of governor who reported directly to the emperor. Recognizing the importance of Judaism to everyday life, Augustus left the highest Jewish judicial body, the Sanhedrin, in charge of Judea's daily affairs.

From that point onward, tensions rose in Judea. The Jews tested Roman patience by refusing to honor the Cult of the Living Emperors. At the same time, the Romans required the Jews to pay increasingly higher taxes. During the rule of a prefect named Pontius Pilate, a group of devout Jews known as the Zealots began to protest Roman rule. The Zealots refused to pay any taxes except for those required by Jewish law. The Romans responded with force. Roman soldiers attacked the Zealots and charged them with treason. The Zealots fought back, ambushing Roman troops whenever they could.

While the Zealots battled Roman troops, a second movement arose in Judea that also called for

The Romans made Herod the king of Judea. After he rebuilt the Temple of Jerusalem, Herod was referred to as "Herod the Great."

the end of Roman rule. This uprising was known as the Messianic movement. Members believed that a leader called the Messiah would unite the Jews and destroy their enemies, ushering in an era of peace and harmony. Ancient Jewish scriptures had promised that such a leader would appear during a time of turmoil and suffering in Judea. To many Jews, the era of Roman rule seemed to be the time foretold by the ancient Jewish prophets.

A Message of Peace

At this moment in history, a Jewish holy man, or Hasid, appeared in a region of Judea called Galilee. His name was Yeshua, or Jesus. Although not an ordained rabbi, Jesus was allowed to speak and teach in the temple and synagogue. He preached change, but not the violent sort practiced by the Zealots. He told his listeners to turn from worldly strife and seek inner peace through prayer and meditation. He urged his followers to love one another and to show kindness to all people, not only to Jews, but also to non-Jews, or gentiles. Teaching by example, Jesus befriended all kinds of outcasts. He even shared meals with the hated tax collectors.

Jesus declared that a new kingdom was being established in Judea. For this reason, some Zealots and members of the Messianic movement thought Jesus would help them drive the Romans from their soil. They were mistaken. Jesus said that his was a spiritual kingdom, not an earthly one. He called this domain the Kingdom of God. When Jews asked him how they should behave toward their Roman rulers, Jesus spoke of peace and cooperation. "Render unto Caesar what is Caesar's," he said, "but render unto God what is God's."

Many Jews found comfort in the words of Jesus. They also were impressed by stories of miracles he had performed. As his fame grew, thousands thronged to see and hear him. When he entered Jerusalem before the feast of the Passover in A.D.

29, he was greeted like royalty. Palm branches were laid before the donkey on which he rode. Some people called out, "King, king."

Crucifixion

Scholars today are not sure what happened next. Christian scriptures state that Jesus was brought before the Sanhedrin and charged with the religious crime of blasphemy, that is, the belief that one is godlike. According to biblical accounts, Jesus did not deny these charges. As a result, the high priest sentenced him to death. Some modern scholars doubt this story. They believe that while Jesus may have been questioned before the Sanhedrin, it was the Roman prefect, Pontius Pilate, who sentenced him to death. What is certain is that Jesus of Nazareth was nailed to a wooden cross with his

Jesus of Nazareth attracted huge crowds with his message of hope and his reputation as a miracle worker.

Jesus was crucified by Roman soldiers outside Jerusalem. This seemingly unimportant action set off a chain of events that changed the Roman Empire and, some say, led to its fall.

limbs outstretched. In this position, Jesus' lungs slowly filled with fluid, causing a slow and painful death by suffocation.

After Jesus' death, his followers continued to spread his teachings. They also claimed that their teacher had risen from the dead. Others denied the story, claiming that Jesus' followers had stolen his body from its tomb. The debate over what happened has lasted for centuries. True or false, the stories about the life and death of Jesus shaped human history, including the history of the Roman Empire.

At first, few people took note of the events in Judea. The number of Jesus' followers was small. Like Jesus, they were devout Jews. Although they preserved their slain leader's memory in a ritual feast of bread and wine, known as the Eucharist, they continued to observe the laws, holidays and rituals of Judaism. Under the guidance of a leader named Peter, Christianity probably would have remained a sect of Judaism. Like most Jews, Peter did not seek converts among the gentiles.

Paul of Tarsus

Another early Christian saw things differently. Paul of Tarsus believed Jesus' message was for all people, Jew and gentile alike. Paul preached this doctrine throughout the eastern half of the Roman Empire. His success was amazing. By the time Paul died around A.D. 67, small groups of Christians were meeting on a regular basis throughout the empire. Paul's letters to these groups were carefully preserved. Later these letters became part of the Christian scriptures.

Paul of Tarsus spread the story and teachings of Jesus throughout the eastern Roman Empire.

Like the Jews, whose scriptures and beliefs they had adopted, the Christians practiced monotheism. Their belief in one god caused the early Christians to reject the Greco-Roman gods and the Cult of the Living Emperors, just as the Jews did. For this reason, many Romans viewed Christians with suspicion. The Christian contempt for ancient Roman rituals seemed disloyal not only to the gods, but to the state, since honoring the gods was an important part of Roman government. The Christians also spoke of a day when Jesus would return to earth and establish a new kingdom. Many Romans took this as a direct threat to the empire.

The Romans misunderstood many Christian beliefs. Because Christians denied the existence of the Greco-Roman gods, for example, some Romans accused them of atheism, or the lack of belief in any god. Since Christians held that all people sinned and needed forgiveness, the Roman philosopher Tacitus concluded that Christians despised the human race. Most disturbing to the Roman mind were rumors about the Christian Eucharist. Christians said they ate the body of Christ and drank his blood during the sacred feast. This led many Romans to conclude that Christians practiced ritual cannibalism.

Persecution of the Christians

At first, the Christians were persecuted in much the same way and for many of the same reasons as were the followers of Christianity's parent religion, Judaism. Many Christians were sentenced to death for failing to offer a sacrifice to the emperor, for example. Christians drew even more Roman wrath than Jews did, because they were more outspoken about their beliefs. They not only refused to take part in pagan (non-Christian) rituals, but declared that no one else should either. While this extreme stance may have won the Christians some converts, it also gained them many enemies.

"The greatest of historians [Gibbon] held that Christianity was the chief cause of Rome's fall."

Will Durant, *The Story of Civilization: Part III, Caesar and Christ*, 1944

"Christianity cannot reasonably be made the villain of the piece."

John P. McKay, Bennett D. Hill, John Buckler, *A History of Western Society*, 1987

For the first two centuries after the birth of Jesus, the number of Roman attacks on Christians rose and fell in waves. The first persecution occurred in Rome after a fire broke out in the city. The emperor, Nero, declared that the fire had been started by Christians. Many Christians were dragged from their homes and put to death. Some were used for Roman amusement. Placed in the gladiator's ring, followers of Jesus had to fight lions with their bare hands. The wild creatures tore the Christians to pieces while Roman mobs cheered.

Nero's decree against Christians applied only to Rome. Elsewhere, the matter of how to treat Christians was left to local authorities. One of these, a deputy in Bithynia named Pliny the Younger, wrote to the emperor Trajan around 112, asking for the emperor's advice on how to treat the Christians.

Many Christians were burned as human torches when Nero blamed them for starting the fire that swept through Rome in A.D. 64.

Trajan believed that Christians caught in the act of worship should be killed, but that Roman soldiers should not be used to hunt down the followers of the new religion.

Trajan's reply was brief and brutal. Christians caught practicing their rituals should be killed, the emperor said. Those who refused to take part in state rituals should be given the chance to renounce their faith. Those who did so should be pardoned; those who refused should be killed. Trajan cautioned Pliny the Younger to take action against Christians only when he had proof of their beliefs, however. He should not accept the word of those who accused others of being Christians, Trajan said, nor should he waste the time of Roman soldiers by sending them to seek out Christians.

Christian Scapegoats

The policy described by Trajan was followed by most emperors and governors for the first two centuries after the birth of Christ. In the third century, attacks on Christians resumed. As in the time of Nero, Christians were blamed for events beyond their control. For the first time since they had set out from Italy to conquer the world, Roman armies began to experience defeats. At the same time, disease swept through portions of the empire. Roman farmers experienced crop failures, which caused food shortages. To the Romans, who believed their pact with the gods had brought them to power, it seemed that the gods were angry. Traditional Romans searched for the cause of the gods' wrath. Some began to wonder if the Christians had provoked the gods. After all, the followers of Jesus made no secret of their contempt for Roman deities. Perhaps the gods were punishing Rome for allowing these heretics to live in the empire.

One of those who accepted this view was Maximinus the Thracian, an emperor who ruled from 235 to 238. He ordered the slaughter of Christians, especially those in Rome and Judea. Before his campaign could get very far, however, Maximinus died. His successors returned to Trajan's less aggressive policy.

As the empire's fortunes continued to shrink, pressure to regain the favor of the ancient Roman gods grew. The emperor Decius, who came to power in 250, was one of those who believed that the empire had to return to its ancient ways to regain strength. Decius revived many pagan rituals. He also decided to stamp out Christianity once and for all. He ordered every person in the empire to publicly worship the state gods. Failure to comply meant death.

The Romans persecuted the Christians on and off for three centuries. Thousands of Christians chose to die rather than renounce their faith.

Some Christians, especially those with great wealth, chose to perform the required ritual rather than be killed. These apostates (those who had abandoned their faith) were given a certificate as proof that they had conformed to Decius' edict. However, many devout Christians chose to die for their faith, becoming martyrs. Others, especially the poor, did nothing, hoping the government would not find them.

Decius died after just one year on the imperial throne, and state persecution of Christians died with him. A few years later, however, the emperor Valerian revived the campaign against them. In 257, he banned all Christian meetings and ordered Christian clergy put to death. Like Decius, Valerian died soon after declaring war on the Christians. After Valerian's death, his son, Gallienus, cancelled his father's decree. For the next forty years, Christians lived in peace.

The last wave of Christian persecution occurred under the emperor Diocletian. A staunch follower of traditional Roman religion, Diocletian had ordered the persecution of the followers of a Persian prophet named Mani in 297. Diocletian turned his attention to the Christians in 303. He ordered their churches destroyed and books burned. He then decreed that all Christian clergy should be arrested and required to make a sacrifice to the state gods. Punishment for those who refused was death. In 304, Diocletian decreed that all Roman citizens must sacrifice to the pagan gods or be killed. Like persecutors before him, Diocletian was struck down soon after issuing his anti-Christian edicts. He became ill in 304, probably suffering a stroke. In 305, Diocletian gave up his throne. Once again, the persecution of the Christians came to an abrupt end.

A Dramatic Change

The fate of the Christians in the Roman Empire changed drastically during the next ten years. Galerius, one of the leaders in Diocletian's four-man rule, or tetrarchy, issued an edict from his deathbed in 311. He declared that Christians could rebuild their churches and reclaim their property. He also stated that as long as they remained orderly, Christians were free to practice their religion. This order, known as the Edict of Toleration, marked a turning point in the empire's history.

An event of even greater importance for Christians occurred one year later on a battlefield near

Constantine's conversion to Christianity marked a turning point in human history. Although less than 10 percent of the population was Christian, Constantine made the new sect the most powerful religion in the empire.

Rome. Constantine, the son of one of the members of Diocletian's tetrarchy, prepared to fight his rival, Maxentius, for control of the western empire. Constantine said that before the battle he had a vision. He saw a giant cross hovering in the sky. At the same time, a voice declared, "By this sign, you shall conquer." Although not a Christian himself, the Roman leader ordered his troops to paint the Greek letters *chi* and *rho*—the first two letters of the Greek word *Christos*, meaning "Christ"—on their shields. He swore that if he won the battle, he would become a Christian. The next day, Constantine's army defeated the forces of Maxentius. Like the Romans of old, Constantine honored the pact he had made with the divine. After being declared augustus by the Senate, Constantine granted Christians complete freedom of worship in the provinces he ruled—Italy, Spain, and North Africa. Once he had defeated his rivals and united the empire in 324, Constantine extended these freedoms across the empire.

Spreading Christianity

With each military success, Constantine became even more confirmed in his religious beliefs. By the time he had gained control of the empire, Constantine reckoned his debt to the Christian god to be enormous. He immediately began to shape the state religion to conform to his own beliefs. Although he accepted the title pontifex maximus when he became emperor, becoming the head of the state religion, Constantine did not perform the pagan rituals associated with this title. Instead, he used his powers to raise the status of Christianity. He declared Sundays to be a Christian holiday. He used state funds to build Christian churches. He had the Christian cross inscribed on Roman coins. He appointed Christians to prominent positions in government and allowed Christian bishops to serve as Roman judges in some areas. In 325, he convened the first council of Christian bishops in Nicaea to decide the basic tenets, or beliefs, of the Christian faith.

As part of his drive to reform the empire, Constantine decided to move its capital from Rome to the ancient Greek city of Byzantium, located in present-day Turkey. One reason for the move was military. Byzantium was easier to defend than Rome, which was easily attacked by sea. Constantine also wanted to make a break with the pagan past, centered in Rome. At the time, most Christians lived in the eastern half of the empire, so it made sense to locate the new capital there. Constantine renamed Byzantium "New Rome" and dedicated it as a Christian city in 330.

Conversions

Constantine did not require pagans to become Christians, or even to honor the Christian god, as the old state religion had required non-Romans to make sacrifices to the state gods. Many Romans did convert to the new religion, however. Many did so out of sincere religious feeling, but others saw conversion to Christianity as an important step to further their careers in Constantine's regime.

Under Constantine, the ancient city of Byzantium became the center not only of Roman government, but also of the Christian church.

For seven years before his death in 337, Constantine used his official powers to discourage the practice of pagan religion. He took treasures from pagan temples and refused to perform pagan rituals.

Constantine did not totally forbid pagan worship, but some of his successors did. In 356, his son Constantius decreed that all pagan temples must close, and those who offered sacrifices to pagan gods should be put to death. This decree was almost identical to the edicts issued by Decius against Christians. In just one century, the oppressed had become the oppressors.

The Roman government's attitude toward Christianity changed drastically a few years later when the emperor Julian assumed power. Raised as a Christian, Julian later became Christianty's most prominent critic.

Constantine used the powers of his office to discourage paganism and promote Christianity. Did this sudden change weaken the Roman Empire and contribute to its fall?

When he became emperor, Julian renounced his Christian faith and restored the worship of the ancient Roman deities.

As a young man, Julian studied Greek philosophies and beliefs. He was especially drawn to the philosophy known as Neoplatonism. Founded by the Greek philosopher Plotinus, Neoplatonism was based on the teachings of Plato, a Greek philosopher who lived from 500 B.C. to 450 B.C. Neoplatonists believed that earthly life is a mere shadow of a more perfect existence known as the One. Plotinus taught that through study and disciplined thought, and with the help of the traditional pagan gods, a person could slowly approach the One. Plotinus believed he had achieved communion with the One, though only a few times.

As an adult, Julian privately renounced his Christian faith in favor of the Neoplatonist philoso-

"[Christianity] had disrupted the unity of the Empire while soldier emperors were struggling to preserve it; it had discouraged its adherents from holding office, or rendering military service; it had preached an ethic of nonresistance and peace when the survival of the empire had demanded a will to war. Christ's victory had been Rome's death."

Will Durant, *The Story of Civilization: Part III, Caesar and Christ*, 1944

"True, many very able minds and forceful characters devoted their lives and energies to the Christian church and not to the empire. . . . Yet the numbers involved in these pursuits were small in proportion to the total population. Furthermore, the Byzantine Empire . . . demonstrated that Christians could handle the sword as well as the cross."

John P. McKay, Bennett D. Hill, John Buckler, *A History of Western Society*, 1987

phy. When he became emperor, Julian made his beliefs public. He overturned the laws against pagans, proclaiming freedom of worship for all faiths. He promoted pagan worship, appointed pagan followers to prominent positions, and encouraged Christians to renounce their faith.

Since most Romans had remained pagan throughout the rule of Constantine and his sons, Julian's revival of paganism met with considerable success, especially in the western half of the empire. Had he lived longer, Julian might have slowed the growth of Christianity. As it was, he died in battle after just three years on the throne. He was the last pagan emperor Rome would see.

A Christian State

From Julian's death onward, the Roman Empire increasingly became a Christian state. In 380, Theodosius I made Christianity the official state religion. During his reign, the Christian emperor ordered the building of several magnificent churches and monuments in the holy city of Constantinople. From the Christian capital, Theodosius tried to unite the empire behind his faith. He outlawed pagan worship and persecuted Christians who preached doctrines that varied from his own.

The successors of Theodosius were more tolerant of other religions, but they all were devout Christians. It was during this Christian reign, less than a century after the death of Theodosius, that the barbarians overran the western half of the empire. Some historians, especially Edward Gibbon, have argued that Christian rule caused the fall of Rome. They point out that while the Christian virtues of patience, meekness, and compassion might contribute toward a serene earthly existence, they are hardly the virtues required to subdue conquered peoples or ward off invading barbarians.

In addition, these historians contend, the quick change in the official state religion caused many loyal pagan Romans to feel estranged from their government. When Christian emperors like Constantius and Theodosius persecuted pagans, this estrangement turned to resentment and even hatred.

At the very least, the turmoil over the official state religion distracted leaders from the day-to-day business of running the empire. The energy spent as the empire shifted back and forth between paganism and Christianity in the fourth century meant that other pressing problems, such as the economy, were ignored. The waves of religious persecution also sapped the empire of valuable resources, both human and financial.

A Fatal Move

Perhaps the most serious result of the rise of Christianity was Constantine's decision to move the capital from Rome to Constantinople (Byzantium). Diocletian had already divided the empire in half, but this change affected only the machinery of government. Constantine's move affected the very meaning of Roman citizenship. Although the ancient Roman Republic had been left behind more than three centuries before, the Roman ideal of a self-governing people guided by the pagan deities had endured into the fourth century A.D. The Roman Empire based on this ideal came to a sudden end under Constantine. To some scholars, the fall of the Roman Empire came not in 464, but 130 years earlier, when Constantine put an end to the pagan cult of the state and moved the capital to Byzantium.

Edward Gibbon saw the impact of Christianity on the empire as more gradual, but no less fatal. He argued that Christianity discouraged the intellectual life, the art, and the creativity that propelled Roman civilization forward. Other scholars disagree. Richard Haywood writes, "The amount of intellectual energy and ability displayed by the Christian writers of the fourth century is astonishing. Pure theology, their prime subject, was pursued with energy, force, and subtlety. The traditional oratorical [public speaking] techniques were successfully applied to sacred oratory [speech]. Poetry of a Christian inspiration made its appearance." Haywood

The writings of Saint Ambrose seem to contradict the idea that the rise of Christianity led to a decline of Roman thought and culture.

points out that two of the most important Christian writers, Saint Augustine and Saint Ambrose, lived in the fourth century. Rather than deadening Roman culture, Christian writers enlivened it. Indeed, the debate between Christians and pagans was one of the most vigorous aspects of Roman arts and letters.

The theory that Christianity weakened the Roman Empire is contradicted by two major historical facts. The first is that the eastern half of the empire, the more Christian half, did not collapse when Rome fell. Indeed, the Christian empire shaped by Constantine and Theodosius remained intact for another thousand years after the sacking of Rome. If Christian virtues generally weaken governments, these historians ask, why did the eastern half of the empire prosper so long?

The second fact is that many of the invading Germanic tribes were Christians, too. Christianity did not seem to weaken them.

Did Christianity Strengthen the Empire?

Some scholars go so far as to claim that Christianity actually strengthened the empire and helped it remain in control of the Mediterranean area longer than it would have had it remained pagan. These scholars point out that the pagan religions had been losing followers for two or three centuries before Christianity became the official religion of the empire. Skeptics had challenged the very idea that the gods existed or in any way affected human life. Had Christianity not come along, this skepticism could have damaged the fabric of Roman life and undermined the government even more quickly than Christianity did.

Five

Did the Romans Lose Their Moral Strength?

(Opposite page) The Baths of Caracalla were just one of many expensive public baths built by the Romans. As the empire grew rich, the Romans began to spend more time and money on such luxuries.

Edward Gibbon and other scholars have argued that a change in moral values caused by the rise of Christianity weakened the Roman Empire, causing it to collapse. Other writers, including some who lived during the Roman Empire, agree that a change in the empire's moral climate led to its fall, but they do not believe the Christian values of meekness and humility are to blame. Rather, they point to another kind of moral decay, one that preceded the Christian revolution. According to this theory, success spoiled the Romans. The abundance of wealth secured through conquest caused them to become slothful, coarse, and uncreative. Over time, they lost the discipline that had built the empire. These changes sent Rome spinning into a destructive cycle. In his book *On the Government of God*, Salvian, a Roman writer and Christian priest, wrote:

> They [the Romans] reclined at feasts, forgetful of their honor, forgetting justice, forgetting their faith and the name they bore. There were the leaders of the state, gorged with food, dissolute with winebibbing, wild with shouting, giddy with revelry, completely out of their senses, or rather, since this was their usual condition, precisely in their senses. If my human frailty permitted, I should wish to shout beyond my

strength, to make my voice ring through the whole world: Be ashamed, you Roman people everywhere, be ashamed of the lives you lead. No cities are free of evil haunts, no cities anywhere are free from indecency, except those in which barbarians have begun to live.

The Grain Dole

According to Duncan Taylor, author of *Ancient Rome*, the trouble began during the Roman Republic, while Gaius Gracchus served as tribune from 124 to 122 B.C. By this time, thousands of poor people had migrated to Rome from the Italian countryside, hoping for a better life in the capital. Most were disappointed. Living in squalid tenements, the poor subsisted on whatever scraps of food they could find or steal. Famine swept through the city several times. To prevent starvation during these food shortages, the government provided free grain to the needy. After the famine had passed, however, the poor had to fend for themselves. Hunger was common.

Gaius Gracchus believed the government should feed the poor of Rome. As in so many areas, the Roman attitude on this was influenced by Greek models. By the second century B.C., it had become common for governments in Greek cities to control the food supply to prevent famine. Such a policy, Gaius Gracchus believed, was in the best interest of the Roman state. Properly fed, the poor would be less likely to riot or steal. They also would feel greater loyalty to the government. Gaius Gracchus also hoped to win the support of poor plebeians. At the time, many plebeians depended on handouts from wealthy senators for survival. By feeding the masses himself, Gaius Gracchus hoped to weaken the ties between the senators and the plebeians.

Gaius Gracchus proposed a law, known as *lex frumentaria*, that allowed poor Romans to buy grain from the government at a low price. The law required that a certain amount of grain be set aside each month for the purpose of feeding the Roman populace. The process of managing the food supply created many new jobs for unemployed Romans, further increasing Gaius Gracchus' popularity among the poor.

Gaius Gracchus was not the only tribune to use grain to enhance his political power. Twenty years after lex frumentaria had been enacted, Lucius Appuleius Saturninus reduced the price of grain to the plebeians, increasing his popularity among the poor and strengthening his position in the Roman government. A few years later, a tribune named Marcus Livius Drusus reduced the price of grain even further. When Caesar Augustus came to power, he began to provide grain free of charge.

During the *Pax Romana*, or great Roman peace, life was easy for many Romans. Did the lack of hardship cause the Romans to become lazy?

At first, the grain dole helped unite the Roman people. It reinforced the idea that in the republic, all people—including the plebeians—shared in the state's success. As Rome became richer, tribunes like Gaius Gracchus argued, it was only proper to use its wealth to banish hunger from its streets.

A Magnet for the Poor

Most Romans viewed the grain dole as an extension of the rights the plebeians had acquired in the republic. Certainly Gaius Gracchus and the other tribunes who developed the grain dole portrayed it as such. Of course, these tribunes had been elected by plebeians, and they were using the cheap grain to buy votes. Even so, few Romans challenged the notion that cheap grain was a legitimate benefit of Roman citizenship.

Although begun with the best of intentions, the grain dole ultimately became a problem, Duncan Taylor and other critics say. Once it became widely known that cheap grain was available in Rome, thousands of poor people flocked to the city from the Italian countryside. As a result, Rome's population swelled. Instead of reducing the number of poor and hungry people, the grain dole had the opposite effect. It increased the number of poor within the city. By the second century A.D., half a million Romans were receiving free grain.

A bigger population meant that those who sought jobs faced more competition. With work nearly impossible to find, many Romans turned to crime and prostitution to make a living. Roman streets became less safe, leading the consuls, and later the emperors, to increase the number of police in the city. Each year the dole became more expensive, not just because the number of recipients grew, but because the costs of maintaining order among the idle poor also grew. The dole's rising cost ate away at the state treasury. In hard economic times, this burden weakened the government even further.

The dole's evils were not merely financial, Taylor and others have argued. These historians maintain that the availability of free food weakened the work ethic of the people. Knowing they could survive without working, people who received the dole had no reason, desire, or drive to do anything. They sponged off society, rather than contributing to it. Children raised on the dole grew up never seeing their parents employed, so they never learned the value or purpose of work. Whole generations were raised to believe the government owed them a living, but they owed neither the government nor their fellow citizens anything.

A Weakening Effect

As the number of the idle poor grew, some Romans began to question the wisdom of the grain dole. Those who worked hard at menial jobs resented the fact that they were scarcely better off than those who did not work at all. Members of the middle and upper classes became angry that their taxes were spent to feed able-bodied people who showed no interest in bettering themselves or Roman society. The dole created a rift between the classes. It also fed a growing sense of despair about the wisdom of Roman leaders. As the empire's fortunes declined, these feelings became more intense. The wealthy blamed the poor for the empire's troubles. The dole eroded Roman unity at a time when it was needed most, contributing to the collapse of the empire.

Historians such as William G. Sinnigen and Arthur E. Boak, authors of *A History of Rome to A.D. 565*, doubt that the dole's effect was so severe. They point out that distributing cheap grain was not a general practice throughout the empire. It was confined to the city of Rome. Because the dole was limited to one city, Sinnigen and Boak argue, feelings of disunity were not widespread enough to contribute to the decline of the empire.

"The dole weakened the poor, luxury weakened the rich; and a long peace deprived all classes in the peninsula of the martial qualities and arts."

Will Durant, *The Story of Civilization: Part III, Caesar and Christ*, 1944

"The Caesars had in fact shouldered the dual task of feeding and amusing Rome. Their monthly [food] distributions . . . assured the populace its daily bread. By the shows and spectacles they provided in various public places . . . they occupied and disciplined its [the city's] leisure hours."

Jerome Carcopino, *Daily Life in Ancient Rome: The People and the City at the Height of the Empire*, 1940

Sinnigen and Boak also stress that the amount of money used to pay for the dole was small compared to overall government expenditures. The impact on the treasury was not great enough to have altered the empire's course, they insist.

Bread and Circuses

While historians debate the effect the dole had on the fate of the empire, there is no doubt that it contributed greatly to another practice that many believe weakened the Roman state. That practice was the state sponsorship of games and contests known generally as circuses. The word *circus* is an ancient Latin word meaning "ring" or "racecourse." Even before the founding of the republic, ancient Romans loved to hold horse races and chariot races. The courses where these events were held were called circuses.

As Rome grew, its circuses became more elaborate. The Circus Flaminius, built at the end of the third century B.C., held thousands of spectators. The Circus Maximus, built under Augustus, had seating for 150,000. Games that were once reserved for holidays became nearly daily events in the first century A.D. The reason, most historians agree, was because the emperors needed to find something for the idle poor to do. Like the grain the poor lived on, the circuses were free. Thousands of poor people flocked to the games for entertainment. In the famous phrase of the Roman writer Juvenal, the people only cared about "bread and circuses."

The state sponsored four permanent chariot-racing teams. Each was known by its racing colors: the Red, the Blue, the Green, and the White. The crowds cheered for their favorite teams as the chariots raced around the dirt course 7 times, a distance of about 5 miles. Successful chariot drivers attracted huge crowds of admirers. Perhaps the greatest of these charioteers was Gaius Appuleius Diocles. In a career that lasted 24 years, Diocles raced 4,257

ANNIAE
ARESCVSA

times. He won 1,462 races, roughly a third of his starts. His admirers hailed him as the greatest charioteer of all time.

A Thirst for Blood

The Roman chariot races may sound like wholesome entertainment, but they were not. There were no rules to these barbaric contests. It was perfectly legal to cause an opponent's horses to fall or chariot to overturn. Death was common at the races, and there is no doubt that some Romans cared more about the damage inflicted at a race than they did about its outcome.

Over time, the Romans added other, even more brutal entertainments to their circus events. Human hunters would attack all kinds of captive prey

The Romans loved chariot racing, and Roman artists often depicted these exciting events.

within the ring. Wild boar, bears, and lions were killed for sport. Sometimes the prey would turn predator, killing their human tormentors. Rather than being horrified, the crowds cheered the creatures on.

Eventually, the Roman thirst for blood could only be quenched with human combat. Two warriors, known as gladiators, would face each other in the ring. To make the contest more interesting, combatants were equipped with different weapons. A man armed with a spear, for example, might fight a man outfitted with a net and a dagger. A man with a sword might duel a man with a club or a mace (spiked club). Once he had subdued his opponent, a gladiator would turn to the crowd. If the opponent had fought valiantly, his life might be spared. If not, he would be killed.

A Roman gladiator looks to the crowd to see if his opponent should live or die. Only fallen gladiators who had fought especially well were spared.

Some gladiators were free men—and sometimes women—who loved danger and sought fame. Most gladiators, however, were slaves, criminals, and captured soldiers from foreign lands. If they prevailed in the ring, they might win their freedom. If they failed, they would die. The circuses served as a brutal extension of the Roman justice system. Combat in the ring often was the sentence for committing a crime. For those who fell in battle, death became the sentence even for a petty crime. The circus ring also served as a vast torture chamber for criminals and others, such as Jews and Christians, who were sentenced to death. These involuntary gladiators, allowed no weapons to defend themselves, seldom escaped with their lives. This "justice" was administered without humaneness and without dignity. The masses cheered each wound and fall.

A Culture of Violence

No one was shielded from these events. Cheers from stadiums could be heard across the capital. Parades of gladiators and condemned prisoners

Criminals sentenced to death often met their end in the circus ring, where they faced wild beasts with nothing but their bare hands.

Saint Augustine believed the circuses played an important role in the decline of Roman culture.

crowded the streets. What effect, if any, did this state-sanctioned bloodshed have on the minds of the Roman people? What lessons did it teach about the value of human life? How did viewing human torture and death on a daily basis affect the viewer?

Saint Augustine, the Christian bishop of Hippo and the author of *Confessions* and *The City of God*, believed that the circuses debased and corrupted those who watched them. Some modern researchers agree. Various studies have shown that people who view violent films in a controlled setting are more willing to accept certain acts of violence than are people who are shown films that do not contain violence. This suggests that Romans who viewed violent acts in the circus may also have become hardened to violence outside the ring. In this way, Roman circuses may have contributed to the development of a coarse, bloodthirsty culture. In such a society, criminals, police, soldiers, and ordinary citizens resorted to violence without regret. Such a culture, some historians believe, was doomed to disintegrate, since it failed to perform government's main task: to protect its citizens from harm.

A Civilized Society?

Other historians dispute the theory that circuses hardened and corrupted the Roman people or had any effect on the empire. They argue that life around the world at that time was equally harsh and barbaric. The Romans only seem more bloodthirsty than other people, these historians maintain, because we know more about their lives. Their entertainments seem especially coarse because in so many other ways their society was civilized. The Romans provided free food and medical care to the poor, had a reasonably fair criminal justice system, patronized the arts, and were great builders. Furthermore, there is no proof that Roman society became any more brutal after the games became popular, these historians maintain.

The funds that supported public entertainments came from the public treasury. The sums spent on circuses rose and fell, depending largely on the attitude of the person who ruled. Some emperors attended the circuses often and lavished state money on them. Hadrian, for example, sponsored a six-day gladiatorial contest that involved 3,670 combatants. Such extravaganzas cost huge amounts of money.

Circuses were not the only unnecessary drain on the Roman treasury. Some emperors spent incredible amounts of money for their own entertainment or glory. Gaius Caesar, known as Caligula, was perhaps the most notorious spendthrift in history. When he came to the throne in A.D. 37, the Roman treasury contained 2.7 billion sesterces, the standard Roman monetary unit. In less than two years, Caligula had spent all of it. Some of this money funded worthy projects, such as the construction of roads and buildings, but most of it was squandered to fulfill the emperor's whims.

(Left) Hadrian spent huge amounts of public funds on gladiatorial contests. Caligula (right) emptied the Roman treasury to pay for elaborate palaces, barges, and banquets.

Tales of Caligula's excesses are legendary. He built a new palace of the finest marble and decorated it with jewels and gold. He also built pleasure barges replete with baths, gardens, and banquet halls. He spent 10 million sesterces on one banquet, an amount of money roughly equal to 3 million dollars today.

Caligula gorged himself not only on rich foods, but also on feasts of human sacrifice. He sponsored countless circuses in which thousands of combatants died.

Out of pride, or perhaps madness, Caligula believed himself divine. He insisted that others address him as *dominus*, or "lord," and that he be worshiped as a god. He declared his sisters to be deities as well. He ordered that statues of himself replace those of Jupiter in Roman temples and shrines, at state expense. He also had a bridge built between Palatine Hill and Capitoline Hill, so that he could more easily confer with his brother god, Jupiter.

Unrestrained Pursuit of Pleasure

Caligula was not the only emperor to empty the state treasury. Nero duplicated the feat during his reign (A.D. 54-68). Like Caligula, Nero spent a portion of the money on roads and public buildings, especially after a fire destroyed two-thirds of Rome in 64. But he also staged elaborate theatrical performances to show off his lyre-playing and poetry-reciting skills. According to legend, Nero was engaged in such a performance when the famous fire broke out in Rome, giving rise to the expression that he "fiddled while Rome burned."

As the empire became wealthier, not only the emperors but also many rich Roman citizens began to luxuriate in their success. Each patrician tried to outdo the other in an ongoing contest of banquets and orgies. The pursuit of pleasure replaced the hard work and discipline that had built the empire in the first place. Some historians maintain that this decay

"Rome fell, not gradually but in headlong course, from virtue toward vice. The old discipline was deserted and the new introduced. The state turned from vigilance to sleep, from military affairs to pleasures, from work to leisure."

Velleius Paterculus, *History of Rome*, A.D. 50

"Did Hellenism and new social customs corrupt the Romans? Perhaps the best answer is this: The Roman state and the empire it ruled continued to exist for six more centuries."

John P. McKay, Bennett D. Hill, John Buckler, *A History of Western Society*, 1987

in the moral character of the patricians led to the weakening of the Senate and the collapse of the republic. It also caused conflict with those emperors who sought to reverse the decline and instill discipline within Roman society.

Although the modern-day image of fat Romans lolling about in their baths and gorging themselves at huge feasts is popular, many historians believe it is exaggerated—a cartoon version of what life was really like in Rome. There is no doubt that thousands, even millions, of feasts were held during the six centuries that Rome ruled the world. It is not clear how the pursuit of such pleasures affected the day-to-day operation of the state.

Nero spent vast sums of money to restore Rome after the fire of A.D. 64. An amateur poet and musician, he also used public funds to stage performances of his poetry and music.

Many members of the Roman upper class gave lavish feasts and banquets. Some experts believe the money spent on these entertainments helped the Roman economy; others say it weakened it.

No doubt, imperial excesses stirred anger and contempt among the people, especially the soldiers. The most wasteful leaders, including Caligula and Nero, were overthrown by the Praetorian Guard. But it is hard to see how spending, no matter how lavish or wasteful, weakened the empire, since such monies continued to circulate within the Roman economy. If anything, the emptying of the state treasury and the squandering of wealth by the patricians may have stimulated the Roman economy and improved the financial health of the empire.

Perhaps the most damaging excesses occurred during the rule of Constantine. Although his extravagances were dedicated to the glory of God, they placed an enormous strain on the treasury. The building of the new capital in Byzantium and the construction of Christian churches throughout the realm depleted the Roman treasury at a time when the empire was already in financial trouble. Because of this spending, some historians argue, the empire could not afford to maintain an army and infrastructure—roads, bridges, and aqueducts—capable of repelling outside attacks.

Slavery

Some historians believe another aspect of Roman life weakened the empire more than the excesses of the wealthy or the gruesome entertainments of the masses. That is the institution of slavery.

Slavery was common in the ancient world. The Bible, for example, depicts times when the entire Jewish population was pressed into slavery—first in Egypt, then in Babylon. The Romans took slaves whenever they conquered a new land. Prisoners from North Africa, Spain, Gaul, Greece, Syria, Judea, and Egypt streamed into Rome. Not only the wealthy, but even the middle class, owned slaves.

Two female slaves help a Roman woman adorn herself. Many Roman families owned slaves.

Some historians believe that buying and selling human slaves devalues human life and corrupts society. Did the slave trade help bring about Rome's fall?

Critics of slavery maintain that it weakens the enslavers by its very nature. Since slaves do most of the work in a society, the slave owners naturally become lazy and corrupt. The work ethic dissolves, and the excess of leisure time leads, inevitably, to crippling vices. Furthermore, the entire idea of viewing another human being as a piece of property distorts a person's sense of values.

The presence of slaves deprived many free Romans of finding gainful employment. Without slaves, there would not have been a need for a grain dole, nor for the brutal games that entertained the idle poor, because jobs would have been more plentiful.

This negative view of slavery grows mainly from the American experience with the practice, according to historians like William G. Sinnigen and Arthur E. Boak. Roman slavery was very different from American slavery, they argue, and perhaps not as corrupting. One difference was that Romans did not view their slaves as racially inferior, so they did not treat them with the contempt with which white Americans treated their African slaves. Indeed, many Romans freely admitted that their slaves were in some cases more refined than they were. Greek slaves were especially prized for their knowledge. Many were given the task of tutoring Roman children.

Roman slaves could earn their freedom through a process of manumission, and a surprisingly high number did so. It is a measure of the bonds that formed between Roman slaves and their masters that many freed slaves continued to live with—and even be buried with—their former masters.

Not all masters were kind, however. Some, especially those in Sicily, were cruel. In 135 B.C., Sicilian slaves revolted, killing many slave owners. In Italy, a slave named Spartacus led the revolt of 70,000 slaves.

Spartacus, a slave trained in the gladiatorial arts, led a revolt of 70,000 slaves. Some historians look upon this event as proof that Roman slavery was a severe institution that was hated by the slaves.

A member of a gladiator school in Capua, Spartacus convinced other slaves to fight their way to freedom. The rebels hid in the forests of Mount Vesuvius and began to band together with other runaway slaves. Two Roman praetors, magistrates ranking just below the consuls, sent armies to subdue the rebels. The ex-slaves defeated both forces. They then moved southward, adding to their numbers as they overran the cities of Campania and Lucania.

Defeating the Rebels

The Roman consuls soon realized it would take the complete force of the Roman army to defeat the rebel slaves. The slaves divided into two armies, one following Spartacus and the other following a fellow member of the gladiator training school, Crixus. Crixus was defeated by the consuls at Apulia. Spartacus, however, overthrew the pursuing consuls as he tried to make his way to his homeland, Thrace. His followers refused to leave Italy, so Spartacus reversed his direction and moved into southern Italy.

Concerned that Spartacus might succeed in freeing all of Italy's slaves, the Senate appointed Marcus Licinius Crassus as commander of the Italian armies. Crassus pursued Spartacus to Bruttium and surrounded his troops. Spartacus and his followers managed to break through Crassus' lines, but Crassus pursued and overtook the rebels. Spartacus died in battle. Six thousand of his followers were captured by Crassus. Each was sentenced to death, condemned to hang on a cross as an example to other slaves who might think of fighting for their freedom.

The revolt led by Spartacus was the last major slave uprising in Rome. Some historians believe that the revolt improved the conditions of slaves in Rome. It did not, however, hasten the end of slavery in the empire. Even the Christians accepted slavery as a part of life when they seized power five centuries later.

Some historians believe that no single practice—neither the grain dole, the blood sports, the excesses of wealth, nor slavery—by itself destroyed the empire. Taken together, however, these vices may have led to a general moral decline that weakened the state.

Other scholars remain unconvinced. They point out that all of these practices existed during the period of Rome's greatest strength, the *Pax Romana*. It was not Romans' behavior that caused the fall of their empire, scholars contend. It was forces outside their control.

Six thousand of Spartacus's followers were crucified as an example to other slaves that slave revolts would not be tolerated in the Roman Empire.

Six

Did Disease Defeat the Romans?

In 1983, Jerome O. Nriagu, an environmental scientist with the National Water Research Institute in Ontario, Canada, published an article about the fall of Rome in the *New England Journal of Medicine*. Nriagu theorized that the decline of the empire had its roots not in the decay of Roman ideals and morality, but in the decay of their bodies and health. The cause of this decay, Nriagu wrote, was chronic lead poisoning.

A soft gray metal that is plentiful in nature, lead was used by the Romans to make many household items. Roman metallurgists blended lead with tin to make a silver-gray metal known as pewter. Craftsmen used the handsome metal to make cups, plates, spoons, cooking pots, and wine vessels. Because lead melts easily, Romans used it to solder cooking utensils made of other metals. They also applied melted lead to copper vessels in the belief that a lead coating enhanced the flavor of foods and drinks.

A Devastating Ingredient

What the Romans did not know is that lead is one of the most poisonous metals a person can ingest. It damages small tubes in the kidneys through which uric acid normally passes. The trapped acid is

(Opposite page) The Romans ate and drank with tableware that was contaminated with lead. Could lead poisoning be blamed for the decline of Rome?

Roman metallurgists blended lead with tin and silver to make ornate tableware. Beautiful to look at, the eating utensils may have been deadly to use.

absorbed into the bloodstream, causing a disease called gout. Lead also blocks the release of an enzyme that helps break down guanine, a substance found in many foods linked to gout. Besides causing gout, lead poisoning has symptoms of its own, including gastric disorders, constipation, insomnia, and numbness.

Every time the Romans cooked with or ate or drank from lead utensils, trace amounts of the deadly metal entered their bodies. When they drank wine that had been treated with a special grape syrup, they ingested even more. The syrup was added to the wine to improve its bouquet and stop the process of fermentation. To make the syrup, Romans boiled grape juice in leaded containers for hours. "One teaspoon of such syrup would have been more than enough to cause chronic lead poisoning," reported Nriagu.

Widespread Contamination

Gout is rare today, yet ancient Roman writers such as Juvenal and Martial mentioned the disease often. In fact, so many ancient writers referred to gout that Nriagu concluded the disease must have been rampant in the empire. He theorized that the emperor Caligula, who showed signs of madness shortly after becoming emperor, may have suffered from lead poisoning. Claudius, too, exhibited symptoms of the disease. He staggered when he walked, slurred his speech, and slobbered.

Indeed, the entire Roman upper class probably suffered from lead poisoning, Nriagu wrote, since patricians consumed large amounts of food and wine. He estimated that the average patrician drank one to five liters of wine per day. Wealthy Romans were more likely to own pewter tableware and lead-coated cookware. They also consumed more spices than the lower and middle classes. The consumption of spices was dangerous, Nriagu found, because merchants sometimes added granules of lead to spices to increase their weight. That way, the merchants could charge more money than the spices were really worth.

Were Caligula's acts of torture and humiliation the result of an evil mind? Jerome O. Nriagu believes they may have been signs of chronic lead poisoning.

If the entire upper class of Romans suffered from lead poisoning, then the disease may have affected the course of Roman history.

Could widespread poisoning of upper-class individuals have affected the direction of the entire Roman state? Many historians believe so. In his book *Civilization and Disease*, Henry E. Sigerist described the process by which disease influences history. Sigerist wrote:

> To the individual, disease is not only a biological process but also an experience, and it may well be one that very deeply affects his entire life. Since man is the creator of civilization, disease, by affecting his life and actions, has influence on his creations also.

Disease, moreover, sometimes attacks not merely single individuals but entire groups; either temporarily in epidemics, or for long periods of time in endemics, when a disease has taken firm hold on a group or region. The cultural life of such groups cannot but reflect the influence of the disease.

According to Nriagu, this is what happened in Rome. Chronic lead poisoning contributed to countless bad—or even mad—decisions on the part of emperors, governors, senators, and Roman generals. Rooted in disease rather than in reason, these decisions did not serve the best interest of the state. Taken together, they led to the decline of the mightiest empire the ancient world had ever seen.

Lead poisoning also may have contributed to another problem known to have plagued the latter years of the empire: succession. The failing health of many emperors caused them to give up the throne.

Other scholars dispute Nriagu's theory. They point out that the skeletal remains of ancient Romans do not contain especially large amounts of lead. Nor does Nriagu's theory explain why the western half of the empire fell while the eastern half did not. Nriagu contends that lead poisoning and gout were present across the empire. If so, some historians wonder, why did they only affect western policies?

Deadly Diseases

A worse threat to the empire, some historians believe, was posed by different diseases: smallpox and the plague. Smallpox is a deadly disease that usually kills one out of four people who contract it. When it swept through the empire in A.D. 167, it killed two thousand people a day. The emperor Marcus Aurelius was one of the victims.

There are two types of plague, bubonic and pneumonic. Bubonic plague infects the lymph glands, causing large abscesses, or buboes, to form. Death is caused by septicemia, or blood poisoning.

"The loss of people through . . . the plague probably made itself felt well into the fourth century. . . . In this machineless economy a loss of population definitely meant a loss of strength."

Richard Mansfield Haywood, *The Myth of Rome's Fall*, 1958

"In 167 A.D. . . . plague swept through the empire and apparently killed large numbers of people. There was ample time for the empire to recover from this plague."

John P. McKay, Bennett D. Hill, John Buckler, *A History of Western Society*, 1987

Pneumonic plague attacks the lungs, causing them to fill with fluid. The lack of oxygen causes the heart and lungs to fail. When this happens, the body turns dark. For this reason, pneumonic plague is often referred to as Black Death.

Plague is caused by a bacteria that attacks rodents. Fleas that have bitten an infected rodent can then transmit the disease to a human being by biting him or her. The disease can then pass between humans.

Plague swept through the Roman Empire several times. One epidemic raged for fifteen years, from A.D. 250 to 265. It is unclear how many people within the empire died, but similar plagues in Europe during the Middle Ages killed from a quarter to a third of the population.

Such a sudden and great loss of life can devastate a society. A lack of laborers can lead to poor

Epidemics of the plague and smallpox swept through the Roman Empire several times, leaving millions dead.

harvests, inadequate planting, and widespread food shortages. With fewer people to buy and sell things, trade slows to a trickle and entire fortunes can dry up. Fewer mine workers can slow the production of precious metals, creating a shortage of public funds.

A Dwindling Population

Unlike warfare, which is generally confined to the adult male population, disease attacks everyone. Because so many women and children die in an epidemic, the population does not rebound as quickly as it does when men alone die. With fewer women to bear and raise children, the effects of an epidemic can last for several generations. The empire may not have been fully recovered from the smallpox epidemic of 167 when the plague struck less than a hundred years later.

Plague claimed the life of Emperor Claudius in 270. This able general had led the Roman armies in several successful campaigns to win back territories that had been lost during the third century. His death was just one of many that weakened the empire in the third and fourth centuries. The loss of hundreds of thousands, perhaps millions, of able-bodied citizens dealt the empire a blow from which it was unable to recover, some historians believe.

Others disagree. John P. McKay, Bennett D. Hill, and John Buckler, coauthors of *A History of Western Society*, wrote, "It is a serious error to conclude that the ravages of disease in the second century were responsible for later catastrophes." The loss of life from smallpox and plague was serious, they believe, but not fatal to the empire. "Even severe epidemics have only a short-term economic effect, after which conditions quickly return to normal themselves," they wrote. The empire still held enough people to maintain a healthy economy and an adequate defense. Indeed, the Roman population still exceeded the numbers of the invaders that poured through Roman borders and sacked the capital.

"Epidemics of major proportions decimated the population under Aurelius, Gallienus, and Constantine. In the plague of 260-265 almost every family in the Empire was attacked; in Rome, we are told, there were 5000 deaths every day for many weeks."

Will Durant, *The Story of Civilization: Part III, Caesar and Christ*, 1944

"Population did decline in the third and fourth centuries. . . . Even so, the population of the Roman Empire outnumbered the invading barbarians, and there were more than enough people to defend the empire."

John P. McKay, Bennett D. Hill, John Buckler, *A History of Western Society*, 1987

Seven

Were the Barbarians Stronger than the Romans?

In A.D. 410, a tribe known as the Visigoths sacked Rome, stripping gold and jewels from the temples and palaces, stealing precious artwork, taking what they wanted from the merchants' stalls and from the workshops of fine craftspeople. Most people refer to the Visigoths and the other tribes that overran the Roman Empire as barbarians. The implication was that members of these tribes were stupid and crude. In fact, they were neither.

Visigoth Culture

The Visigoths and other Germanic tribes had a very different society from that of the Romans, however. They did not build or live in great cities, as Romans did. Instead, they lived in small groups scattered about the land, raising crops and livestock. Each tribe had rules and taboos that were passed down from one generation to the next, but they lacked the body of written law that held Roman society together. Councils of elders, not courts, settled disputes. The so-called barbarians enjoyed story telling and poetry, but they did not have theaters or literature as the Romans did. Tribal art was meant to be worn or used, not just looked at. Tribal artisans decorated jewelry, weaponry, pottery, and clothing. They did not erect statues, paint murals, create mo-

(Opposite page) The Huns, a fierce nomadic people, forced the tribes of northern Europe to retreat toward the borders of the Roman Empire.

saics, build fine buildings, or create other art for its own sake. In many ways, the culture of the Germanic tribes resembled that of the Romans themselves before they had encountered the Etruscans and Greeks.

Perhaps the greatest strength of the Germanic tribes lay in their attitudes toward battle and heroism. Combat was cherished, considered nearly divine. Germanic boys were raised to be warriors, not merchants or government officials. They competed in contests of hunting and battle skills. The strongest warriors usually became the leaders. There were few weak-willed or enfeebled leaders of northern tribes. Most were men of strength and courage. The people they led were not paid soldiers, but blood relatives, fiercely loyal to tribe and leader.

Pressure from the Huns

Toward the end of the fourth century, a nomadic, or wandering, Asian people, the Huns, swept across the plains of Russia and into eastern Europe. The Huns were every bit as fierce as the Visigoths and even more numerous. When they invaded Visigoth territory, the Visigoths retreated to the Danube River, which formed the northern border of the Roman Empire. The Visigoth leaders turned to the Romans for help. They offered to help the Romans fight the approaching Huns if the Romans would allow them to cross the Danube and settle in Roman territory.

The soldiers at the border knew the Visigoth request was important. They forwarded the offer through the chain of command. Finally it reached the emperor, Valens. A former soldier, Valens saw wisdom in gaining the aid of the hard-fighting Visigoths. Although no one knew it at the time, Valens' decision proved to be one of the most important political decisions made in the history of the empire, for it began a series of events that led directly to the collapse of the western half of the Roman Empire.

"With gloomy fear the sons of the Mediterranean [the Romans] looked upon these giants [the Gauls], with their long red hair and huge moustaches. They were a wild warrior folk who trampled down whatever stood in their way."

Eduard Meyer, *Geschichte des Altertums*, 1975

"If the army had been guarding the borders instead of creating and destroying emperors, none of these invasions would have been possible."

John P. McKay, Bennett D. Hill, John Buckler, *A History of Western Society*, 1987

As the Huns attacked Europe, Valens decided to unite with the Visigoths to repel the invaders. The strategy worked, but the Romans failed to form a strong bond with their new allies.

Under the terms of the agreement, the Visigoths were to give up their weapons as they crossed the Roman border. Those who wished to fight for Rome would be issued new weapons. The plan went awry, however. The Roman officers at the border let it be known that they would accept bribes in exchange for allowing the Visigoths to keep their weapons. As a result, the Visigoths settled within the empire fully armed with their weapons of choice.

A Missed Opportunity

Once inside Roman borders, the Visigoths were treated badly by the Romans. The Romans charged the new settlers excessively high prices for food. They made the Visigoths settle on small parcels of poor land. Through these actions, the Romans turned their potential friends into enemies. In 378, the Visigoths rebelled against Roman rule. Visigoth warriors and Roman soldiers met on a battlefield near Adrianople. Using their own tactics and weapons, the Visigoths won.

The emperor Valens died in the battle of Adrianople. His successor in the east, Theodosius, made peace with the Visigoths by allowing them to more or less rule themselves. Unlike other peoples that had been absorbed into the Roman Empire, the Visigoths did not accept Roman laws or customs. Their alliance with Rome was purely military. They did not participate in the Roman state nor did they expect the Romans to interfere with their lives.

Theodosius used the Visigoths not only to resist the Huns, but also to fight the Persians and other tribes of Goths. When civil war broke out in A.D. 383, Theodosius enrolled even more Visigoths to fight the army of Maximus, who had seized control of the west. With the Visigoths' help, Theodosius prevailed. By the time he died in 395, however, more than half the Roman army was made up of Germanic tribesmen. These warriors used their own traditional weapons and fought only for Visigoth officers. They were an army within the army, as future emperors were to find out.

Rebellion

After Theodosius died, the Visigoths elected one of their nobles, Alaric, as their king. By uniting behind one ruler, the Visigoths believed that they could force Rome to grant their demands for more

A Roman coin depicts Theodosius, who made peace with the Visigoths by allowing the Germanic tribe to rule itself.

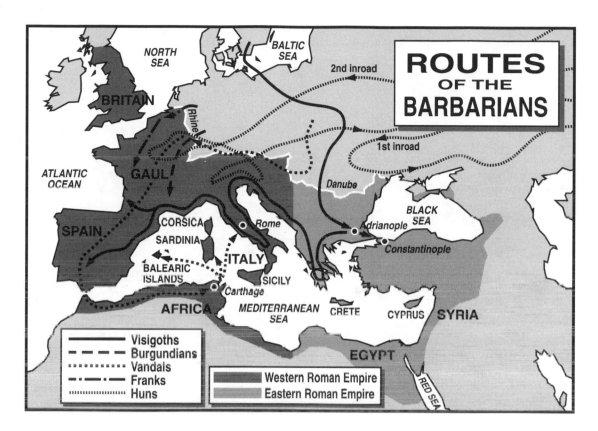

ROUTES OF THE BARBARIANS

and better land. The Romans ignored Visigoth demands, so Alaric led his army against them.

Each time the two forces clashed, the Visigoths were defeated, but the Roman commander Stilicho, who was himself a member of a northern tribe, the Vandals, allowed the Visigoths to retreat.

At the same time he was fighting the Visigoths, Stilicho went to war with forces in the eastern empire over the control of Illyricum (the Balkans). With his soldiers engaged on two fronts, Stilicho was unable to react when news reached him in 406 that four barbarian tribes—the Asding, the Siling Vandals, the Suevi, and the Alani—were crossing the Rhine into Gaul. Since the Visigoths would not help him repel the invaders, there was nothing Stilicho could do to stop the invasion.

The Franks made Roman Gaul their new home in A.D. 406. Engaged in a war with forces from the eastern Roman Empire, Stilicho could do nothing about the invasion of the Franks and other Germanic tribes.

With the Rhine border broken, other Germanic tribes poured into Gaul, including the Franks and the Burgundians. As the tribes settled in Gaul, they pushed the Visigoths further south. Angry at Rome's broken promises, Alaric of the Visigoths led his people toward the capital city on a mission of revenge. There was nothing Stilicho or anyone else could do. In their brief alliance with the Romans, the Visigoths had learned all about Roman fighting formations, strategies, and battle plans. The warlike Visigoths swept aside Roman resistance and entered the marble-crowned capital in 410.

Alaric then led his forces south. His plan was to cross the Mediterranean and settle in northern Africa, which was known as a land rich in grain. The Visigoths built a large number of ships, but a huge storm destroyed the fleet. Shortly after the disaster, Alaric died.

Alaric's brother, Athaulf, led the Visigoths back to Gaul. He promised the emperor, Honorius, that the Visigoths would again serve the Roman Empire. Honorius rejected this bid for peace, so the Visigoths moved on to Spain. There, a Visigoth warrior named Wallia murdered Athaulf and seized control of the tribe.

A Bargain with Rome

Like Alaric, Wallia dreamed of leading his people to Africa. Once again the Visigoths built a fleet, and once again a storm wrecked their ships and their plans. The Roman emperor, Constantius, offered the Visigoths food and land if they would help the Romans in their campaign to drive out the tribes that had invaded in A.D. 406. Wallia agreed, and the Visigoths moved against the other Germanic tribes that had settled inside the Roman Empire.

Wallia and his tribesmen defeated the Alani and the Siling Vandals and made peace with the Suevi and the Asding Vandals. This time, Rome stuck to its bargain, granting land to each of the remaining tribes. Many Romans were moved off their land to make way for the Germanic settlers.

In 429, Boniface, the Roman governor of North Africa, asked the Siling Vandals to settle in his province. He badly needed the support of hard-fighting forces, and the Vandals quickly agreed. Once in Africa, the Vandals took charge of the province. They used the rich land not only for farming, but as a base for piracy in the Mediterranean. By the middle of the fifth century, their raids on passing ships and on the coastal cities of Europe had greatly disrupted Roman trade. The waters that for eight centuries the Romans had called "our sea" had fallen into foreign hands. In 455, the Vandals sacked Rome itself.

The Vandals sack Rome in A.D. 455. The Roman armies were powerless to stop them.

The Vandals stole what remained of Roman wealth and finery. They also destroyed much of the city.

The western Roman army was so weakened that the emperor had no choice but to enlist more Germanic tribes for the empire's defense. When an Asian warrior named Attila the Hun led his people in an assault on Gaul in A.D. 451, it was the Visigoths and the Franks who repelled him. By the middle of the fifth century, the armies of Gaul, Spain, and Italy were under the control of the Germanic soldiers.

When a Roman general named Romulus Augustulus deposed the emperor Nepo in 475, the emperor in the east had no choice but to call upon the barbarian forces to overthrow him. A German master soldier named Odoacer led his tribesmen to Rome and defeated the forces of Romulus Augustus. Nepo was restored to the throne, but only in name. Odoacer actually controlled the armed forces of Italy. With the Vandals in charge of Africa, the Germanic tribes in charge of Spain and Gaul, and Odoacer in command of Italy, the Roman domination of the west had come to an end.

When Attila the Hun and his forces attacked Gaul, the Romans had no choice but to turn to the Germanic tribes for help. By 451, the Germanic tribes controlled Gaul, Spain, and Italy.

"The Germans who were now peopling north Italy and filling the army were physically and morally superior to the surviving native stock."

Will Durant, *The Story of Civilization: Part III, Caesar and Christ*, 1944

"If the Romans had left the Greeks to their own devices and had applied themselves to the consolidation of their rule in the west, they might have created a compact and homogeneous *bloc* of Latin-speaking peoples which would have been impregnable to all assailants."

Max Cary, "The Roman Empire: Retrospect and Prospect"

Some historians believe that the western half of the Roman Empire did not decline and fall. Instead, it was conquered. André Piganiol, a French historian, wrote: "The Empire did not die a natural death. It was assassinated." In the so-called barbarians, Rome had met its political and military match. On land and on sea, the Romans were simply outfought by stronger, more energetic forces.

Too Many Concessions

Other historians disagree. In their view, the empire was not conquered, it was given away. The concessions made to the Germanic invaders were too great, these historians suggest. Richard Mansfield Haywood writes:

> It might have been desirable to acquire this new strain of population had it been possible slowly to assimilate the Germans and make them Romans as had been done with many other peoples, but the stubborn preference of the Germans for their own social values and the fact that they were admitted in large homogeneous groups was bound to raise difficulties.

Haywood points out that the Germanic invaders were never required to serve in the imperial army. Instead, they fought only for their own leaders. As a result, northern tribes never felt any real loyalty to Rome. They also were not required to pay the usual taxes to the state treasury. Therefore, Spain and Gaul, which had once contributed to Roman wealth, simply stopped doing so. The lack of revenue from the west greatly weakened the empire.

"One People"

The greatest strength of the Roman Empire had been the ability of its leaders to make the people living within its borders feel as though they belonged to the world's first superpower. The ancient Roman poet Claudian wrote:

Rome alone has taken the conquered to her bosom as a mother, not a ruler, and she has cherished the whole human race under one name. She has called the conquered her citizens and gathered them in the wide-flung net of her devotion. To her way as peacemaker we all owe the fact that the newcomer may live as if in his own land, that a man may change his home, that men may go to Thule for pleasure and penetrate what once was fearful wilderness, that we may drink of the Rhone or the Orontes, that we are all one people.

The leaders of Rome failed to convince Germanic invaders that they were part of "one people." It was this inability to create a bond with the invaders, rather than the inability to repel them, say Haywood and other historians, that led to the ruin of the west. The fall of Rome was a political, not a military, failure.

Epilogue

The Legacy of Rome

Was it government, religion, dissipation, disease, or the barbarians who caused the fall of Rome? Historians avidly continue to debate that question.

And some dispute the notion that the Roman Empire fell at all. "The fall of empires? What can that mean?" asked the French historian Abbe Galliani in 1744. "Empires being neither up nor down do not fall. They change appearance." Galliani had a point. Those who lived in the Italian countryside in the years after A.D. 476 would not have noticed any major change in the government. Those living in Spain and Gaul under Germanic kings would not have noticed anything either. Gradually these kings and other powerful nobles increased their influence, forming the kingdoms of Europe.

Remnants Everywhere

In this view, medieval Europe had its roots in the late Roman Empire and grew from it. Several European languages—the Romance languages—evolved from the language of the Romans, Latin. English, too, was shaped by Latin words and rules of grammar. Medieval legal codes grew from Roman laws. The remnants of Roman literature, art, and architecture were rediscovered in the period known as the Renaissance and have influenced

countless artists and scholars ever since. Roman representative government served as a model for the framers of the Constitution of the United States, who named one of the houses of Congress after the ancient Roman body, the Senate.

Roman civilization did not disappear when the city fell. Many of Rome's best qualities lived on in Europe and traveled to the New World. In some ways, we remain Rome's citizens today.

The glories of Rome live on in western art, architecture, language, and law.

For Further Exploration

Ian Andrews, *Pompeii*. Cambridge: Cambridge University Press, 1978.

Isaac Asimov, *The Roman Empire*. Boston: Houghton Mifflin, 1967.

Lionel Casson, *Daily Life in Ancient Rome*. New York: American Heritage, 1975.

Ron Goor and Nancy Goor, *Pompeii: Exploring a Roman Ghost Town*. New York: Thomas Y. Crowell, 1986.

Jill Hughes, *Imperial Rome*. New York: Gloucester Press, 1985.

Anthony Marks and Graham Tingay, *The Romans*. London: Usborne, 1990.

Don Nardo, *The Roman Empire*. San Diego: Lucent Books, 1994.

Don Nardo, *The Roman Republic*. San Diego: Lucent Books, 1994.

Works Consulted

Crane Brinton, John B. Christopher, and Robert Lee Wolff, *Civilization in the West*. Englewood Cliffs, NJ: Prentice-Hall, 1973.

Robert Graves, *Greek Gods and Heroes*. New York: Dell, 1965.

Richard Mansfield Haywood, *The Myth of Rome's Fall*. New York: Thomas Y. Crowell, 1958.

John P. McKay, Bennett D. Hill, and John Buckler, *A History of Western Society*. Boston: Houghton Mifflin, 1987.

Henry E. Sigerist, *Civilization and Disease*. Chicago: University of Chicago Press, 1962.

William G. Sinnigen and Arthur E. Boak, *A History of Rome to A.D. 565*. New York: Macmillan, 1977.

Duncan Taylor, *Ancient Rome*. New York: Roy, 1960.

F.W. Wallbank, *The Awful Revolution*. Toronto: University of Toronto Press, 1969.

Index

About the Author

Bradley Steffens is the author of eleven books for young people. He was first encouraged to write about history by his sixth grade teacher, Betsy Crawford. She suggested that he turn his hobby of making newspaper front pages into extra credit history reports. He produced seven such newspapers, covering topics from "Socrates Drinks Hemlock" to "Rosetta Stone Deciphered." Mrs. Crawford made copies of each paper for the class—the author's first published works.

Picture Credits

The Elephant's Child

from the JUST SO STORIES

BY RUDYARD KIPLING

Illustrated by Tim Raglin

ALFRED A. KNOPF PUBLISHERS • NEW YORK

This is a Borzoi Book Published by Alfred A. Knopf, Inc.

Copyright © 1986 by Random House, Inc., and Rabbit Ears Productions
All rights reserved under International and Pan-American Copyright Conventions.
Published in the United States by Alfred A. Knopf, Inc., New York,
and simultaneously in Canada by Random House of Canada Limited, Toronto.
Distributed by Random House, Inc., New York.

MANUFACTURED IN THE UNITED STATES OF AMERICA

4   6   8   10   9   7   5

Designed by Antler & Baldwin Design Group

Library of Congress Cataloging-in-Publication Data
Kipling, Rudyard, 1865–1936. The elephant's child.
Summary: Because of his insatiable curiosity about what the
crocodile has for dinner, the elephant's child and
all elephants thereafter have long trunks.
(1. Elephants—Fiction) I. Raglin, Tim, ill. II. Title.
PZ7.K632E1   1986b   (E)   85-377
ISBN 0-394-88401-9   ISBN 0-394-88300-4 (book/cassette)

As adapted by Joel Tuber for the video version of
THE ELEPHANT'S CHILD
narrated by Jack Nicholson
directed by Mark Sottnick

To Chuck and Mary Alice

On the High and Far-Off Times the Elephant, O Best Beloved, had no trunk. He had only a blackish, bulgy nose, as big as a boot, that he could wriggle about from side to side; but he couldn't pick up things with it.

But there was one Elephant—a new Elephant—an Elephant's Child—who was full of insatiable curiosity, and that means he asked ever so many questions. *And* he lived in Africa and filled Africa with his insatiable curiosities.

He asked his tall aunt, the Ostrich, why her
tail-feathers grew just so, and his tall aunt Ostrich
spanked him with her hard, hard claw.

He asked his tall uncle, the Giraffe, what made his skin spotty, and his tall uncle, the Giraffe, spanked him with his hard, hard hoof.

And still he was full of insatiable curiosity!

He asked his broad aunt, the Hippopotamus, why her eyes were red and his broad aunt, the Hippopotamus, spanked him with her broad, broad hoof; and he asked his hairy uncle, the Baboon, why melons tasted just so, and his hairy uncle, the Baboon, spanked him with his hairy, hairy paw.

And *still* he was full of insatiable curiosity!

He asked questions about everything he saw, or heard, or felt, or smelt, or touched, and all his uncles and aunts spanked him.

And still he was full of insatiable curiosity.

One fine morning in the middle of the Precession of the Equinoxes this insatiable Elephant's Child asked a new fine question that he had never asked before.

He asked, "What does the Crocodile have for dinner?" Then everybody said "Hush!" in a loud and dreadful tone, and then they spanked him immediately and directly, without stopping, for a long time.

By and by, when that was finished, he came upon a Kolokolo Bird sitting in the middle of a wait-a-bit thorn-bush and said, "My father has spanked me, my mother has spanked me, and all my aunts and uncles have spanked me for my insatiable curiosity; and I *still* want to know what the Crocodile has for dinner!"

Then the Kolokolo Bird said, with a mournful cry, "Go to the banks of the great gray-green, greasy Limpopo River, all set about with fever-trees, and find out."

That very next morning, when there was nothing left of the Equinoxes, because the Precession had preceded according to precedent, this insatiable Elephant's Child took a hundred pounds of bananas (the little short red kind), and a hundred pounds of sugar-cane (the long purple kind), and seventeen melons (the green crackly kind), and said to all his dear families, "Good-bye. I am going to the great gray-green, greasy Limpopo River, all set about with fever-trees, to find out what the Crocodile has for dinner." And they all spanked him once more for good luck, though he asked them most politely to stop.

Then he went away, a little warm, but not at all astonished, eating melons and throwing the rind about because he could not pick it up.

He went from Graham's Town to
Kimberley, and from Kimberley to
Khama Country, and from Khama
Country he went east by north, eating
melons all the time till at last he came
to the banks of the great gray-green,
greasy Limpopo River, all set about
with fever-trees, precisely as the
Kolokolo Bird had said.

$\mathcal{N}$ow you must know and understand, O Best Beloved, that till that very week, and day, and hour, and minute, this insatiable Elephant's Child had never seen a Crocodile, and did not know what one was like. It was all his insatiable curiosity.

The first thing that he found was a Bi-Colored-Python-Rock-Snake curled round a rock.

" 'Scuse me," said the Elephant's Child most politely, "but have you seen such a thing as a Crocodile in these promiscuous parts?"

"Have I seen a Crocodile?"
said the Bi-Colored-Python-Rock-Snake,
in a voice of dreadful scorn. "What will
you ask me next?"

" 'Scuse me," said the Elephant's Child,
"but could you kindly tell me what he has
for dinner?"

Then the Bi-Colored-Python-Rock-
Snake uncoiled himself very quickly from
the rock, and spanked the Elephant's Child
with his scalesome, flailsome tail.

"That is odd," said the Elephant's Child, "because my father
and my mother, and my uncle and my aunt, not to mention
my other aunt, the Hippopotamus, and my other uncle, the
Baboon, have all spanked me for my insatiable curiosity—and
I suppose this is the same thing."

So he said good-bye very politely to the Bi-Colored-
Python-Rock-Snake, and helped to coil him up on
the rock again, and went on, a little warm, but not at all
astonished, eating melons, and throwing the rind about
because he could not pick it up, till he trod on what he

thought was a log of wood at the very edge of the great gray-green, greasy Limpopo River, all set about with fever-trees.

But it was really the Crocodile, O Best Beloved, and the Crocodile winked one eye—like this.

" 'Scuse me," said the Elephant's Child most politely, "but do you happen to have seen a Crocodile in these promiscuous parts?"

Then the Crocodile winked the other eye and lifted half his tail out of the mud, and the Elephant's Child stepped back most politely because he did not wish to be spanked again.

"Come hither, Little One," said the Crocodile. "Why do you ask such things?"

" 'Scuse me," said the Elephant's Child most politely, "but my father has spanked me, my mother has spanked me, not to mention my tall aunt, the Ostrich, and my tall uncle, the Giraffe, who can kick ever so hard, as well as my broad aunt, the Hippopotamus, and my hairy uncle, the Baboon, *and* including the Bi-Colored-Python-Rock-Snake, with the scalesome, flailsome tail, just up the bank, who spanks harder than any of them; and *so*, if it's quite all the same to you, I don't want to be spanked anymore."

"Come hither, Little One," said the Crocodile, "for I am the Crocodile," and he wept crocodile tears to show it was quite true.

Then the Elephant's Child grew all breathless and panted, and kneeled down on the bank and said, "You are the very person I've been looking for all these long days. Will you please tell me what you have for dinner?"

"Come hither, Little One," said the Crocodile, "and I'll whisper."

Then the Elephant's Child put his head down close to the Crocodile's musky, tusky mouth, and the Crocodile caught him by his little nose, which up to that very week, day, hour, and minute, had been no bigger than a boot, though much more useful.

"I think," said the Crocodile—and he said it between his teeth, like this—"I think today I will begin with the Elephant's Child."

At this, O Best Beloved, the Elephant's Child was much annoyed, and he said, speaking through his nose, like this, "Led go! Led go! You're hurtig be!"

Then the Bi-Colored-Python-Rock-Snake scuffled down from the bank and said, "My young friend, if you do not now, immediately and instantly, pull as hard as ever you can, it is my opinion that your acquaintance in the large-pattern leather ulster"—and by this he meant the Crocodile—"will jerk you yonder into limpid stream before you can say Jack Robinson."

This is the way Bi-Colored-Python-Rock-Snakes always talk.

Then the Elephant's Child sat back on his little haunches and pulled, and pulled, and pulled, and his nose began to stretch.

And the Crocodile floundered into the water, making it all creamy with great sweeps of his tail, and *he* pulled, and pulled, and pulled.

And the Elephant Child's nose kept on stretching; and the Elephant's Child spread all his little four legs and pulled, and pulled, and pulled, and his nose kept on stretching; and the Crocodile threshed his tail like an oar, and *he* pulled, and pulled, and pulled, and at each pull the Elephant Child's nose grew longer and longer—and it hurt him hijjus.

Then the Elephant's Child felt his legs slipping, and he said through his nose, which was now nearly five feet long, "This is too buch for be!"

Then the Bi-Colored-Python-Rock-Snake came down from the bank and knotted himself into a double-clove-hitch round the Elephant Child's hind legs, and said, "Rash and inexperienced traveler, we will now seriously devote ourselves to a little high tension, because if we do not, it is my impression that yonder self-propelling man-of-war with armor-plated upper-deck"—and by this, O Best Beloved, he meant the Crocodile—
"will permanently vitiate your future career."

That is the way all Bi-Colored-Python-Rock-Snakes always talk.

So he pulled, and the Elephant's Child pulled and the Crocodile pulled; but the Elephant's Child and the Bi-Colored-Python-Rock-Snake pulled hardest; and at last the Crocodile let go of the Elephant Child's nose with a plop that you could hear all up and down the Limpopo.

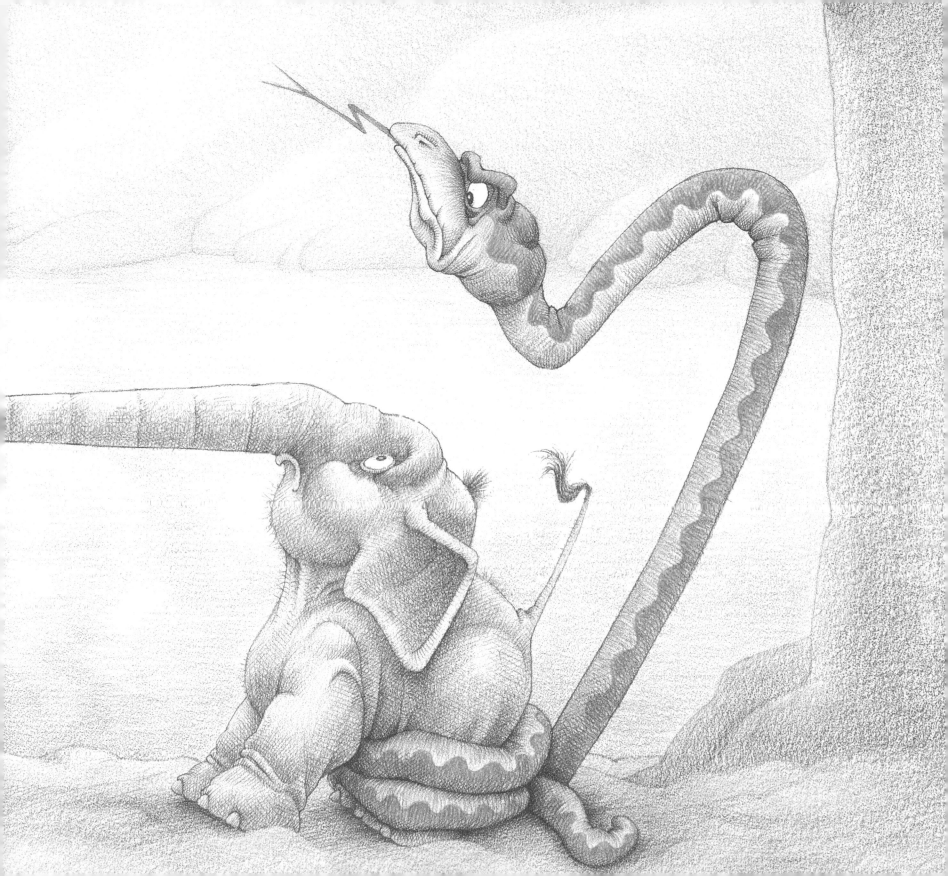

Then the Elephant's Child sat down most hard and sudden; but first he was careful to say "Thank you" to the Bi-Colored-Python-Rock-Snake; and next he was kind to his poor pulled nose, and wrapped it all up in cool banana leaves, and hung it in the great gray-green, greasy Limpopo to cool.

"What are you doing that for?" said the Bi-Colored-Python-Rock-Snake.

" 'Scuse me," said the Elephant's Child, "but my nose is badly out of shape, and I'm waiting for it to shrink."

"Then you will have to wait for a long time," said the Bi-Colored-Python-Rock-Snake. "Some people do not know what is good for them."

The Elephant's Child sat there for three days waiting for his nose to shrink. But it never grew any shorter, and besides, it made him squint. For, O Best Beloved, you will see and understand that the Crocodile had pulled it out into a really truly trunk same as all Elephants have today.

At the end of the third day a fly came and stung him on the shoulder, and before he knew what he was doing he lifted up his trunk and hit that fly dead with the end of it.

" 'Vantage number one!" said the Bi-Colored-Python-Rock-Snake. "You couldn't have done that with a mere-smear nose. Try and eat a little now."

Before he thought what he was doing the Elephant's Child put out his trunk and plucked a large bundle of grass, dusted it clean against his forelegs, and stuffed it into his own mouth.

" 'Vantage number two!" said the Bi-Colored-Python-Rock-Snake. "You couldn't have done that with your mere-smear nose. Don't you think the sun is very hot here?"

"It is," said the Elephant's Child, and before he thought what he was doing he schlooped up a schloop of mud from the banks of the great gray-green, greasy Limpopo and slapped it on his head, where it made a cool schloopy-sloshy mud-cap all trickly behind the ears.

" **'Vantage number three!**"
said the Bi-Colored-Python-Rock-Snake.
"You couldn't have done that with a mere-smear nose.
Now, how do you feel about being spanked again?"
" 'Scuse me," said the Elephant's Child,
"but I should not like it at all."
"How would *you* like to spank somebody?"
said the Bi-Colored- Python-Rock-Snake.
"I should like it very much indeed,"
said the Elephant's Child.
"Well," said the Bi-Colored-Python-Rock-Snake,
"you will find that new nose of yours very useful to
spank people with."
"Thank you," said the Elephant's Child.
"I'll remember that; and now I think I'll go
home to all my dear families and try."

So the Elephant's Child went
home across Africa frisking and
whisking his trunk.

When he wanted fruit to eat he pulled fruit down from a tree, instead of waiting for it to fall as he used to do. When he wanted grass he plucked grass up from the ground, instead of going on his knees as he used to do.

When flies bit him, he broke off the branch of a tree and used it as a fly whisk; and he made himself a new, cool, slushy-squishy mud-cap whenever the sun was hot.

When he felt lonely
walking through Africa,
he sang to himself down his
trunk, and the noise was
louder than several brass bands.
He went especially
out of his way to find a
broad Hippopotamus
(she was no relation of his),
and he spanked her very
hard, to make sure that
the Bi-Colored-Python-
Rock-Snake had spoken
the truth about his new
trunk. The rest of the
time he picked up the
melon rinds that he had
dropped on his way to
the Limpopo—for
he was a Tidy
Pachyderm.

One dark evening he came back to all his dear families, and he coiled up his trunk and said, "How do you do?" They were very glad to see him, and immediately said, "Come here and be spanked for your insatiable curiosity."

"Pooh," said the Elephant's Child. "I don't think you peoples know anything about spanking; but *I* do, and I'll show you."

Then he uncurled his trunk and knocked two of his dear brothers head over heels.

"O Bananas!" said they. "Where did you learn that trick, and what have you done to your nose?"

"I got a new one from the Crocodile on the banks of the great gray-green, greasy Limpopo River," said the Elephant's Child. "I asked him what he had for dinner, and he gave me this to keep."

"Looks very ugly," said his hairy uncle, the Baboon.

"It does," said the Elephant's Child, "but it's very useful." And he picked up his hairy uncle, the Baboon, by one hairy leg, and hove him into a hornet's nest.

Then that bad Elephant's Child spanked all his dear families for a long time, till they were very warm and greatly astonished.

He pulled out his Ostrich aunt's tail-feathers; and he caught his tall uncle, the Giraffe, by the hind leg and dragged him through a thorn-bush; and he shouted at his broad aunt, the Hippopotamus, and blew bubbles into her ear when she was sleeping in the water after meals.

But he never let anyone touch the Kolokolo Bird.

*A*t last things grew so exciting that his dear families went off one by one in a hurry to the banks of the great gray-green, greasy Limpopo River, all set about with fever-trees, to borrow new noses from the Crocodile.

When they came back nobody spanked anybody anymore; and ever since that day, O Best Beloved, all the Elephants you will ever see, besides all those that you won't, have trunks precisely like the trunk of the insatiable Elephant's Child.